Let Me Tell You a Story

Tony Campolo

WORD PUBLISHING
NASHVILLE
A Thomas Nelson Company

Let Me Tell You a Story

Copyright © 2000 Tony Campolo

Scripture quotations are from The Holy Bible, King James Version.

Library of Congress Cataloging-in-Publication Data

Campolo, Anthony.
    Let me tell you a story / by Anthony Campolo
      p. cm.
    ISBN 0-8499-4205-5 (pbk.)
    1. Homiletical illustrations. I. Title.

BV422.2 .C34 2000
251'.08—dc21   00-34985
                                                                  CIP

Printed in the United States of America
00 01 02 03 04 05 PHX 9 8 7 6 5 4 3 2

Dedicated with hopes and prayers
to
Naomi Ruth Goodheart,
My newest granddaughter,
Whose story is about to be told

Contents

Preface

Preface

Over the years, I have written twenty-six different books. In them I have told a lot of stories to illustrate the ideas and concepts I was trying to communicate. I'm not sure that people remember my concepts and ideas, but I'm very aware that my readers remember my stories. Many have utilized them in sermons or teaching situations. I have also collected scores of stories that I have never utilized in sermons or in my writings. I got to thinking that it would be a good idea to put all these stories together in one book. And so I did.

I want you to feel free to use these stories at will. Needless to say, I would like you to provide credit where credit is due, but it would be a source of encouragement to my ministry if I knew that these stories were being used to drive home truth and illuminate the messages of those who seek to communicate the gospel.

Since I am primarily a speaker, rather than a writer, I want to give a bit of advice on how to use stories.

The same story can be utilized to illustrate a host of different truths. As you come across stories in this book, do not think they can only be used to address the subjects indicated by the topic headings under which they fall. With some solid employment of the imagination, you will be able to use many of these stories to highlight points and illustrate truths other than the ones for which I have employed them.

In telling a story, you will have to do a lot of practicing in order to be effective. Often my listeners think I am telling a story for the very first time because I work hard at seeming spontaneous, as ironic as that sounds. Timing is everything in the telling of a story. The pauses, facial expressions, hand gestures, and the speed at which the story is told, all must be carefully rehearsed if the telling is to be effective.

If the meaning of a story is self-evident after making the application, move on. Explaining a story at length can make your communication seem didactic.

One final warning! No story or illustration perfectly or completely reveals the truth it is intended to convey. Please don't use the stories as though they were full explanations of what I believe and what I think. In most instances, these stories convey the best of the truth as I understand it, and in some rare cases they may evidence more. As you read them, ENJOY! I hope they get you to laugh and cry and *feel* the messages of the gospel with increased passion.

The Bible says that no man "liveth to himself, and no man dieth to himself." And so it is with the writing of books. In the writing of this one, special thanks must go to Valerie Hoffman. She spent huge amounts of time typing out the contents of what you read. Unlike any other book I have written, this one was put together almost completely via dictation. Valerie had the unenviable task of listening to my voice droning on for hours from dictation tapes. If you like this book, please stop and give her a special round of applause.

TONY CAMPOLO
Eastern College
St. Davids, Pennsylvania

Introduction

My mother was a storyteller. She was the very best. She kept the family entertained at dinner, and though she told the same stories over and over again, we never tired of listening to her. That was because they were never exactly the same. The words she used, the descriptions she provided, the detailed exchange of comments between the characters of her stories, seemed better with each telling.

In later life, Mom worked in an old folks' home, and the management of the home was glad to have her because of her storytelling. She could keep old men and women entranced. She was able to carry them out of the mundane setting of the home into a never-never land of wide experiences.

I inherited the propensity for storytelling from my mother, and when I preach, I hardly ever make a point without illustrating it in some way. Sometimes people question the veracity of the stories I tell. On one occasion, some people took my son aside, when he was just a little boy, and asked, "When your father tells those wonderful stories, are they really true? In a lot of them you are the main character. So, tell us, do things really happen the way he says they do?"

My son reflected thoughtfully on the question and answered, "Yes, my dad does tell the truth. But, when I hear him tell the stories, I always have the feeling that he *remembers big!*" To such a charge I will plead guilty, because I often sense extraordinary things in ordinary situations. So far as I'm concerned, that particular practice is what makes stories really good.

When I went off to study at seminary, my professor of preaching was Dr. Norman Paullin. He was one of the most loved preachers in the Philadelphia area. He, more than any other preacher I knew, was able to tell stories in a way that made the listener feel he or she was right there when the events of the story happened. I remember him saying to us once, "My sermons are like the Empire State Building . . . They're just one story on top of another!"

Given my mother's propensity for storytelling, and that Norman Paullin was my homiletics professor, it should come as no surprise to my audiences that the substance of what I communicate day in and day out is generally in the form of stories. One of my critics has said that I use illustrations like a drunk uses lampposts—"more to support his instability than to illuminate his path." He may be right in that accusation. Someone else suggested that I use stories instead of theology as a basis for my sermons, but I must tell you that, in the end, my stories do not illustrate my theology—they *are* my theology. I choose to tell truths about myself, about others, and most of all about God, not with theological statements, but with stories.

Sören Kierkegaard, the Danish philosopher who made existentialist thought seminal to much of Christian theology in the middle part of the twentieth century, would have approved of my approach to communicating truth. He made the point that Jesus preached primarily through storytelling because, according to Kierkegaard, the gospel is not so much heard as it is *overheard!* By that Kierkegaard meant that the Bible is full of stories about all kinds of people, both good and bad, and as the stories of these people are told, we find ourselves. Perhaps a good example of how that really works comes from Henri Nouwen's wonderful sermon on the prodigal son. In that story all of us can identify with the characters as Jesus describes them. Nouwen makes clear that each of us will identify, at one time or another, with each of the story's characters. Each of us can at some time be likened to the prodigal son. We have all wandered away from a father's goodness and adopted a destructive lifestyle, only to discover the futility of it all, and then wanted to go back and set things right. At some other point, each of us acts like the elder brother of the story, exhibiting a holier-than-thou self-righteousness, and showing a reluctance to forgive and offer restoration to the brother or sister who needs it. And ultimately, each of us will have to someday play the role of the father, who will be challenged to show unconditional love and welcome the sinner home again.

According to Kierkegaard, the gospel is always overheard if it is heard at all. A didactic message seldom gets through. Generally, we put up our defenses against direct accusations or directives, and try to ward off truth that is blatantly directed at us. But, says Kierkegaard, when we hear a story about somebody else, and realize that that person's story is also about us, we can, in an unthreatened manner, apply the truth that we overhear in the story to our own life situations.

A friend of mine, Burton Visotzky, who is a Jewish rabbi, conducts seminars for business executives who work in the Wall Street district of New York. Once a week he gathers with such people, and together they study the Book of Genesis. The incredible stories about Abraham and his descendants (which he calls the stories of an incredibly dysfunctional family) are read and discussed in depth. It is the rabbi's contention that these corporate executives have little difficulty finding themselves in the outrageous characters who appear in the Genesis stories. In Abraham they find a man who, even in old age, is able to dream dreams and have visions of starting over again and doing something great. In the deceptions of Jacob they find much that is in their own character. The jealousies and sexual intrigues inherent in the stories mirror experiences in their own lives. My friend believes that the stories in the Book of Genesis were written primarily to enable all of us to reflect on the painful realities of our own lives, and that we will find in them more of ourselves than we are at first ready to admit.

I believe Kierkegaard was right and that my rabbi friend is right today. So much am I convinced that the gospel is overheard, that I have organized this book with that as its major theme. The chapter headings all refer to truth that I believe can be overheard in the stories that are told. The stories give expression to what I believe about God, other people, and about myself. I hope to tell stories that will enable you to overhear some truths about human history, as well as provide some understanding about your own everyday life. Most of all, I hope these stories will help you to understand more clearly what it means to be a person of faith in our post-modern world.

1

What We Overhear about God the Father

Obviously, God is too great for any story to do more than hint as to what the Divine character is all about. It would take an infinite array of stories to reveal all the truth about God. There are those who will correctly point out that even my reference to God as "Father" is an inadequate reference, in that God transcends any of our earthbound understanding of male and female or father and mother. In the words of Sören Kierkegaard, "God is totally other!" All that these stories can do is help us feel something of a truth that cannot be put into words.

Hide-and-Seek

The God we worship is a hidden God. He does not force us to confront Him, but waits patiently for the time to come when we will seek Him out. He longs for us to seek after Him with heart and mind and soul.

A rabbi's child was playing hide-and-seek with some children. She went away and hid herself. But the other children acted cruelly. While she was hiding, they ran away and left her behind.

When the little girl realized she had been abandoned by her friends, she went running home and threw herself into her father's arms and cried, "Daddy, I was hiding and nobody tried to find me!" The father hugged his daughter and said, "God understands. He understands more than you realize."

Indeed, it must be the ultimate frustration of God that we seldom seek Him out. The Bible says that if we truly seek Him, we will find Him.

What God Does

The Jewish people in the ancient world were very different from the Greeks. If you had asked the Greeks what they thought about God, they would have talked about God's essence. They would have said such things as, "God is the ground of all being!" or, "God is the unmoved mover!" They might have used words like "omnipotence," "omniscience," and "omnipresence," in order to describe what God is.

The Hebrew people, on the other hand, did not even try to get at the essence of God. They knew it was past finding out. Instead of talking about what God *is*, the Jews always talked about what God *did*. If you had asked them about God, they would have said, "Our God is the One who delivered us from the hands of the Egyptians and brought us into the Promised Land. Our God is the One who defended us against our enemies, has guided us, and has made us the chosen people." The Jews would have talked about what God has done and is doing and would have contended that all we can know about God is what we can deduce from His *actions*. They knew that they were in a covenant relationship with God, and that God would not break that covenant. They knew that God would go on loving them, no matter what—because of what He had done.

Danny Dutton

Jesus once said that unless we become like little children we will not be able to enter the Kingdom of Heaven. He also said that a little child would lead us. Given these words from Jesus, it might be a good idea to listen to what Danny Dutton, from Chula Vista, California, had to say about God when he was eight years old.

> One of God's main jobs is making people. He makes them to take care of things here on earth. He doesn't make grownups, just babies. I think that's because they are smaller and easier to make. That way

he doesn't have to take up his valuable time teaching them to talk and walk. He can just leave that up to mothers and fathers.

God's second most important job is listening to prayers. An awful lot of this goes on. Some people, like preachers and things, pray other times than just before bedtime. God doesn't have time to listen to the radio or TV on account of this.

Jesus is God's son. He used to do all the hard work, like walking on water and doing miracles, and trying to teach people about God who really didn't want to learn. They finally got tired of him preaching to them and they crucified him. But he was good and kind like his Father, and he told his Father that they didn't know what they were doing, and to forgive them. And, God said, "Okay!" His Dad appreciated everything he had done and all his hard work on earth, so he told him he didn't have to go out on the road anymore. He could stay in heaven. So, he did.

You should always go to Sunday School because it makes God happy, and if there's anyone you want to make happy, it's God. Don't skip Sunday School to do something you think would be more fun, like going to the beach. This is wrong! And besides, the sun doesn't come out on the beach until noon, anyway.

If you don't believe in God, besides being an atheist, you also will be very lonely, because your parents can't go everywhere with you—like to camp—but God can.

It's good to know that he's around when you're scared of the dark or when you can't swim very good and you get thrown in real deep water by big kids. But, you shouldn't just always think of what God can do for you. I figure God put me here and he can take me back anytime he pleases.

And that's what I believe about God.

H₂O

That the doctrine of the Trinity is beyond our understanding is all too obvious. We Christians make the incredible claim that God is in three persons, and yet God is one. This is not only a perplexing statement for Muslims and Jews, but most Christians have difficulty making sense of it. Certainly it is way beyond me. But then I consider water! When water is cooled to below 32° Fahrenheit it becomes a solid, and we call it ice. The properties of ice are very different from the properties of water, yet the chemical formula for ice is H_2O, the same as it is for water. If we take water and heat it up to 212° Fahrenheit it turns to steam, which is a gas.

Obviously, the properties of steam are very different from the properties of water and also very different from the properties of ice. And yet, the chemical formula for steam is H_2O. Isn't it strange, when we think about it, that water, ice, and steam each are very distinct, but are still essentially the same? Perhaps they will help us to understand by analogy that it is one essential God who is expressed in Father, Son, and Holy Ghost.

God Loves

A friend of mine who served a church in a derelict section of the city had to face the fact that his congregation was dwindling toward nothing. People were moving away from the neighborhood or dying, and no new people were moving in. He was only able to survive financially by earning money on the side. For instance, he had an arrangement with some of the local undertakers to take the funerals nobody else would take.

My friend was a saintly pastor and, like all true saints, he did not realize it. He did not recognize the significance of his own life, nor the importance of the stories he could tell about his everyday experiences. Thus, it was always to my advantage to ask about what was going on in his life, because the stories he would never use in his own sermons were stories I could greedily gobble up and use in mine.

On one occasion I asked if he had any good stories to tell me, and he answered with the expected, "No." I zeroed in. "Well, on Tuesday at eleven o'clock in the morning, what were you doing?" I thought that by forcing him to think about some specific point in the past week, he would reveal something he deemed unimportant, but that I would see as incredibly significant.

"Oh! Tuesday at eleven o'clock," he said. "Now that was fascinating. Early that morning the undertaker down the street called me on the telephone and told me he needed somebody to conduct a funeral for a man who had died of AIDS. None of the other ministers wanted to have anything to do with this funeral because of that—and also because there was every indication that all the people who would be attending the funeral would be homosexual."

I asked, "What did you do?"

"I took the funeral," he answered, "and about thirty homosexual men showed up. As I read Scripture, prayed, and spoke, they never once looked up at me. Their heads were bowed. They stared at the floor. They seemed to be afraid of making eye contact with me. I ended up speaking to the tops of their heads.

"When the service was over, we went out and got into the assigned automobiles and followed the hearse out to the cemetery. They stood on one side of the grave, and I stood on the other as the casket was lowered down into the hole that was to be the dead man's grave. I read some more Scripture and said some more prayers.

"As I spoke to these men, they stood like statues, each of them frozen in place. They had dazed expressions in their eyes and seemed to be focused on nothing. They just stood there, without a nerve or a sinew moving.

"After I said the benediction, I motioned to leave, but none of them moved. I turned back and asked, 'Is there anything more I can do for you? Is there anything more I can say?'

"One of them answered, 'Yeah! They usually read the Twenty-third Psalm at these things. You didn't read the Twenty-third Psalm, pastor. Would you mind reading it?'

"And so I read the Twenty-third Psalm to them. Then another of the men said, 'There's something that Jesus said about the Spirit of God blowing and landing anywhere He wants to land, and on anybody. Could you read that part of the Bible to me?'

"I turned to the third chapter of John and read to those men about the Spirit blowing where it listeth like the sound of the wind, but how we cannot know from where it comes or where it is going.

"Then one of them said, 'Pastor! There's a part of the Bible that I really like. It's about how nothing can separate us from the love of God. Do you know what part I'm talking about?' I answered, 'Of course I do!' And I opened my Bible to the eighth chapter of Romans and read to them, 'Neither death nor life, neither angels nor demons, neither the present nor the future, nor any powers, neither height nor depth, nor anything else in all creation, will be able to separate us from the love of God that is in Christ Jesus our Lord.'"

As Jim told me that story, I hurt inside. When I heard about these men hungrily listening to the words that told them there was nothing—NOTHING—that could separate them from the love of God I hurt, because I realized that these men were hungering for God, but they would never set foot inside a church. And I knew why they would never set foot inside a church. They would never do so because they were convinced that church people despised them. And do you know why they believe that church people despise them? It is because church people *do* despise them!

When I tell this story, people often mistakenly assume that I have some unorthodox views about what is acceptable behavior so far as the Bible is concerned. That is not the case. I am not approving of any lifestyle that I think runs contrary to the first chapter of Romans. I am expressing my disapproval of a church that fails to love people that *God will never stop loving!*

God's Children

The God we worship is a God who loves all people of all races and tribes. This is articulated well in a Hasidic story that tells of a great celebration in heaven after the Israelites are delivered from the Egyptians at the Red Sea, and the Egyptian armies are drowned. The angels are cheering and dancing. Everyone in heaven is full of joy.

Then one of the angels asks the archangel Michael, "Where is God? Why isn't God here celebrating?" And Michael answers, "God is not here because He is off by Himself weeping. You see, many thousands of His children were drowned today!"

Things We Want

There are those who say that if God loves us, He should answer our prayers. But we should recognize that sometimes it may be that God doesn't answer our prayers *because* He loves us.

Sören Kierkegaard tells the story of a schoolboy who refuses to learn. His teacher tries hard to get him interested in his schoolwork and to apply himself to his studies. But the boy shrugs off her concerns and pays her little attention. She begs him to cooperate. She pleads with him to let her teach him, but he refuses. He just wants to play.

Eventually the teacher says, "Okay. Tell me what you want to do, and you can do it."

The boy says he would like to just sit in the back of the room and make some drawings and sleep a little bit, and spend some time doing nothing at all. The teacher tells him that he can, and he is allowed to do exactly what he wants.

Kierkegaard ends the story by saying, "The boy got what he asked for because the teacher had given up on him." He then goes on to say, "Beware when God answers prayer!" He suggests that we sometimes get what we want because God has given up on us. On the other hand, God may refuse to give us what we want because He loves us.

This point is especially real to me because of an incident when my own father did not accede to a desperate request. I was about eight years old when I went to a Saturday matinee at the movies and saw a cowboy film about Hopalong Cassidy. I was so impressed with that cowboy hero that I went home and told my father that when I grew up, I wanted to be a cowboy. I really meant it! I was intense! I was passionate about it!

The good news is that my father didn't give me what I wanted. Wouldn't it have been a weird situation if, when I was seventeen and asked him about going to college, he had exclaimed, "College! What do you mean you want money for college? When you were eight you told me you wanted to be a cowboy. You said it with such passion, and you pled with such earnestness, that I made sure your dreams would come true. I spent the money I had saved for you on a thousand acres of land in Texas, along with a horse and a hundred head of cattle. It's all waiting for you, because that's what you pled for. That's what you said you *really* wanted!"

> ⌇ Booker T. Washington once said that he prayed, "God, help me to understand Your mind." And God answered, "Booker, that's a little too much for you to handle. Let's try a peanut."

I'm glad to say that my father did not give me what I thought I wanted when I was eight years old, so that he might one day give me something I really needed. He didn't want me to have what I thought I wanted, because he knew, eventually, it wouldn't be what I wanted at all. And so it is with God.

Working It Out

Sören Kierkegaard tells the story of a boy trying to learn arithmetic. The teacher gives him a book full of problems to solve. In the back of the book there's a listing of the answers to the problems, but the teacher instructs the boy never to look at the answers in the back of the book. Instead, he is to work out the answers for himself.

As the boy does his homework, he cheats. He looks in the back of the book and gets the answers beforehand, finding it much easier to work out the problems if he knows the answers in advance. Kierkegaard points out that while it is quite possible for the boy to get good grades this way, he will never really learn mathematics. As difficult as it may prove to be, the only way to become a mathematician is to struggle with the problems himself, not by using someone else's answers, even if those answers are the right ones.

It's obvious that on life's journey we are faced with problems, and we sometimes wonder why Jesus doesn't just spell out the answers so that we know exactly what to do. According to Kierkegaard, God doesn't give us the answers because He wants to force us to work out the problems for ourselves. It is only by struggling with the problems as they present themselves, day in and day out, that we can develop into the kinds of mature people God wants us to be.

God As the Hound of Heaven

God has been described as the Hound of Heaven. What that means is that there is no way to escape Him. No matter where we go or where we try to hide, when we turn around, there is God. Certainly, that's what David was trying to tell us in Psalm 139:7–8, when he wrote, "Whither shall I go from thy spirit? or whither shall I flee from thy presence? If I ascend up into heaven, thou art there: if I make my bed in hell, behold, thou art there."

Watching over Me with Love

As a boy growing up in the city, it was somewhat dangerous for me to walk to school all by myself. So my mother paid Harriet, a neighborhood girl a few years older than I, to be responsible for getting me to and from school each day. Harriet was paid five cents a day for this service.

As I grew older, I became very conscious of what I believed was an enormous amount of money going into Harriet's hands. So I went to my mother and told her that there was no need for her to pay Harriet any longer, that she should give me the nickel each day, and I would walk myself to school. I assured her that I could do it with no problem at all. I kept on begging and begging until my mother gave in and said, "Okay! If you're very careful, I'll give you the nickel a day, and you can put the money in the bank and save it to buy Christmas presents for your sisters."

That seemed like a good idea. So from that time on I walked myself to school, collected the money, and did not allow the Campolo wealth to leave the household.

Years later, when my mother had passed on, I was at a family get-together with my sisters and I reminded them of my independent spirit, even when I was a child. I reminded them of how I walked myself to school, and how I needed no one's help in getting there and back each day, and how that translated into good presents for them at Christmas time.

My sisters laughed at me and one of them said, "Did you think that you went to school alone and came home alone? Every day when you left the house Mom followed you. And when you came out of school at the end of the day, she was there. She always made sure that you didn't notice her, but she watched over you coming and going, just to make sure you were safe and that nobody hurt you. Didn't it ever occur to you that there was something strange about the fact that when you knocked on the door she didn't answer right away, and that it always took a minute or so before she opened the door of the house to let you in? That's because she would follow you home then sneak in the back door. When she opened the front door and let you in, you were always left with the impression that you had been on your own, when in reality she had been watching over you all the time."

And so it is with God!

The Bus Driver

God being the Hound of Heaven was made clear in a testimony I heard from a man in a church in England. He was a bus driver in London. One day his boss told him that Billy Graham, an American evangelist, had come to town, and that a lot of people had to be bused in from towns and villages around about London, so they could hear him speak at Wimbley Stadium. "My boss told me I was to go pick up some people and bring them in to hear this famous American," he said, "and I did what I was told to do. As people were getting off the bus to go into the stadium, one of them turned and asked, 'Why don't you join us? Why don't you come in and listen to Billy Graham? I'm sure you need what he has to say.' But, I turned down the invitation.

"The following year, I moved to New York City. I got a temporary work visa and again took a job as a bus driver. One day I was told that Billy Graham was going to speak at Madison Square Garden, and that people in communities as far away as Philadelphia were coming to hear him. So, I drove down to Philadelphia and picked up some church folks and drove them up to the Big Apple. As they were getting off the bus, one of them stopped and asked if I would join them. He told me that I would benefit a great deal from what Billy Graham had to say. But I turned him down.

"I married an Australian, and a few years later found myself in Sydney, Australia. Once again, I took a job driving a bus. And once again, I was told that Billy Graham was in town and that I was to drive some church folks to the stadium where the evangelist would be preaching. I did, and as the people were getting off the bus, a man said, 'Why don't you come in with us? It would do *you* a world of good, and it would make *me* very happy. You really need to hear what this man has to say, mate!' I figured there was no escaping it. No matter where I went, I was confronted with this Billy Graham. So I went in to hear him speak. It was then that I fell under conviction and made a decision to give my life to Christ."

We should recognize that our God is a God that will not let us go. He will chase us to the ends of the earth and in love make sure that we have the opportunity to hear His voice, calling us to surrender to Him.

The God of Joy

Do It Again

My friend Earl Palmer, who pastors the University Presbyterian Church in Seattle, Washington, introduced me to the works of Lord

Chesterton. He made me aware of Lord Chesterton's belief that "God may be the only child left in the universe, and all the rest of us have lost our capacity for joy and wonder, because of sin." I picked up that theme from Earl and the suggestion for this story. It's a story built around the question of how God made daisies. Did God just say, "DAISIES, BE!" or did He do it in a childlike way?

I'm a grandfather now. (Grandchildren are God's reward for not killing your own children.) I love to play with my grandson, Roman Campolo, when he comes to visit. When he was just a little tyke, we had a game. I would throw him up in the air, catch him, bounce him off my knee, then set him on the floor. I could always count on him yelling, "Do it again, Pop-Pop! Do it again!" And I would. And each time, he would yell, "Do it again!" with more joy and more enthusiasm than the time before. He never once said, as teenagers do, "Been there. Done that." After doing it fifty times he was all the more exuberant, screaming at the top of his lungs, "Do it again, Pop-Pop! Do it again!!"

And so, I ask again, how did God create daisies? Did He just say "Daisies, be!"? Or after He created the first little daisy, did something childlike inside the heart of God yell, "Do it again!"? So God created daisy number two. And once more, something inside of God said, "Do it again!" And daisy number three was created. And then four, five, and six. And, each time God clapped His hands and shouted, "Do it again! Do it again! Do it again!" And fifty billion trillion daisies later the great God of the universe is still jumping up and down, clapping His hands and yelling, "Do it again! Do it again!"

Once, after telling that story, a dignified man came up to me and said, "I'm offended by your idea that God should be a God of childlike joy. It just seems so inappropriate." I didn't answer the man, but something inside of me said, "Mister, that's what's wrong with your theology."

One More Ride

That our God is a God of joy was certainly understood by my son, Bart, when he was just a little guy. When he was nine years old I took him to Disneyland in California. Nowadays, there's a huge general admission, but back in the old days you bought tickets for the rides you wanted to enjoy.

At the end of the day, as we were leaving, little Bart turned to me and said, "I want one more ride on Space Mountain!" I told him we were out of tickets and out of time. He responded, "Jesus wants me to go!"

Intrigued by his theological claim to be able to read the mind of God, I asked where he got such an idea. He responded, "From you! Sunday, when you were preaching, you said that whenever we cry, Jesus cries. You said that He feels everything we feel. Well, if that's true, then when I'm having a really happy time on the roller coaster, He's really enjoying Himself too. So, I *know* He wants me to have one more ride on Space Mountain!"

That's not bad theology. I am convinced that God so empathizes with us that our emotions are experienced by Him. One of the reasons God sent His Son into the world was because, in feeling the pain and sorrow of our lives so acutely, He wanted us to be relieved of them so that He could be relieved of them. No wonder Jesus said, "I have come that my joy might be in you, and that your joy might be full."

By the way, Bart did get another ride on Space Mountain.

2

What We Overhear about Jesus

Perhaps the most incredible claim we make about the man Jesus, is that He is actually God. We Christians believe that in Jesus, God became one of us, so that we might get a glimpse of what God is all about.

Ants

Imagine a man who loved ants. Out behind his house he had an ant-hill, and every day he would go out and yell at the ants, "I love you! I love you! I love you!" Of course, the ants never got the message since they were ants and he was a man, and humans can't communicate with ants by shouting at them. So the man did something more than just shout. Each day he would bring them sugar, pieces of bread, and other goodies to enjoy. And as the ants devoured the good things he would yell at them, "They're from me. They're from me. I love you, I love you!" Still the ants did not get the message. But in this make-believe story the man had magical powers, and he was able to transform himself into anything he wanted to be. What he wanted to be must seem all too obvious. To communicate with ants there was only one thing to do: transform himself into one of them.

So he did just that! He became an ant and went in among them. He told all the other ants about the goodness of the great man who had hovered over them. He told them how much that man loved them.

The other ants could not help but be curious and asked, "How come you know so much about that man?" To which this special ant replied, "Because I am that man. I became one of you because only by becoming one of you could I communicate how much I care for you, and let you know what I'm really like."

The Prince

In John 1:14 the writer tells us that God became a human being, and that in Him we got a glimpse of what the glory of God is all about. Sören Kierkegaard picked up this theme when he told about a prince who fell in love with a maiden of his kingdom. But he was afraid to go to her as a prince. He thought that if he appeared with all the symbols of majesty, she would be awed and left with no real choice but to marry him. He didn't want her awe. He wanted her love. And so, he took off his princely garments and put on the clothes of a peasant. Then, he went to the marketplace where she worked, got to know her, and wooed her. He went to her as one of her own kind, won her affection, and only then revealed to her who he really was.

There is no doubt that the God who loves us took on our nature and became one of us in order to communicate with us. Who could withstand the glory of the Almighty? God had to empty Himself of that (Philippians 2) and take on the form of a human being. It was through this special human being that the fullness of God was revealed to us. And now we know Him.

The Race

I saw another good illustration of the incarnation in the 1996 Olympics. An American runner, Derek Redmond, was entered in the 400-meter race. For years and years he had practiced for this race, with his father as his trainer and coach.

During his heat, Redmond was well out in front of the pack when his Achilles tendon snapped. He stopped running but did not drop out of the race. In a struggling limp he pulled himself forward, dragging his wounded leg behind him. The crowd stood and cheered the wounded runner on, but the pain was so great and the wound so serious that it was doubtful he could make it. Suddenly, a middle-aged man jumped over the guardrail onto the track, caught up with Derek, put his arms around his waist, and helped him all the way to the finish line. It was his father!

When the race was over, Redmond told the press, "He was the only one who could have helped me, because he was the only one who knew what I'd been through."

And so, the God of heaven comes down alongside each of us to carry us the rest of the way. He is the only One who can, because He is the only One who understands what we've been through and what lies ahead.

The Housewife

My friend and prominent radio preacher Steve Brown eloquently describes a housewife who was washing dishes in the kitchen sink one day after the children had left for school. She looked at one particular plate. She stared at it for a long time and asked over and over again, "How many times have I washed this plate? How many times have I dried it? How many times will I wash it and dry it again?" She then set down the plate, took off her apron, packed a few of her belongings, and left.

That night she called home to tell her husband that she was all right, but that she just could not come home again. From time to time, over the next several weeks, she would call just to see how her husband and children were doing. But she would never tell them where she was, nor accede to the pleas from her family to return.

The husband hired a detective to search for her, and after picking up a few leads, the detective tracked her down. She was in another state, living in a small apartment over a luncheonette where she had a job as a waitress. Her husband set out immediately to bring her home. When he found the place she was staying, he knocked on the door of her upstairs apartment. She opened the door, saw him, and did not say a word. She went into the bedroom, packed her belongings, and silently followed him out to the car. Then, in silence, he drove her back home.

Several hours later when the two of them were alone in their bedroom he finally spoke, and he asked her, "Why didn't you come home before? Over the phone I begged you to return. Why didn't you come?"

The wife answered, "I heard your words, but it wasn't until you came for me that I realized how much you cared and how important I was to you."

It can be said that though the prophets of the Hebrew Bible may have tried to tell us about God's love, we never really got the message until God showed up among us. He broke into history and became one of us, and as one of us, showed us His love.

A True Friend

Through Jesus, God told us that we were His friends. Some hint of what that friendship might be like is found in a commonly circulated story about a couple of soldiers in World War I.

One night, as the struggle settled into trench warfare, a lieutenant commanded his men to sneak across a field and attack the enemy. Obeying the officer's command, the men inched their way out of their safety and began to crawl toward the enemy. Suddenly, gunfire rang out! Bullets flew in almost every direction! The frightened men scurried back to their own trenches as quickly as they could and hunkered down.

When the gunfire ceased it was eerily almost still, except for the moaning and groaning of one of the men who had been left behind on the field, wounded. The man kept crying for his friend George, begging him to come and save him. George, in turn, pled with the young lieutenant to be allowed to go. But the young lieutenant said "No" over and over again, trying to explain that he didn't want to lose another man in what would be an obviously foolhardy rescue attempt. "I've lost him. I don't want to lose you too," the lieutenant shouted. But the young recruit kept pleading and finally, in exasperation, the lieutenant said, "Okay! If you want to get yourself killed, go ahead! I'm tired of listening to your whining. Go out and get yourself killed, if that's what you want to do!"

The young soldier sneaked over the edge of the trench and inched his way along the ground, crawled to his friend, grabbed him, and slowly pulled him back to safety. He got his wounded friend back to the trench, and after pushing him over the edge of the trench, George fell in on top of him. But it was too late—he was dead.

The lieutenant yelled, "George, I told you there was no point to your bravery. Why did you risk your life? You put the entire unit in jeopardy. And for what? There was no point to what you did. You were a fool!"

George answered, "I was no fool. When I got to him he was still alive, and the last words he said were, 'George! I knew you'd come!'"

That's what a friend does. And that's what Jesus did for us. In our despair and hopelessness, He left the safety of heaven and came to us, and took us into His haven of rest.

What He Did for Us

When we talk about what Jesus did for us on the cross, there are many dimensions to be explored. When He died on that tree and took the punishment for our sins, He provided deliverance for us. On Judgment Day, we need not be threatened with the fear of condemnation, for as it says in Romans 8:1, "There is therefore now no condemnation to them which are in Christ Jesus."

And there's more good news about what Jesus did for us! Not only did He take the punishment for our sins, but He forgets that we ever sinned in the first place. To tell the truth, I would not want to go to heaven if God remembered. I can imagine showing up and having God say, "Campolo! We've been waiting for you!" Thank God, that when we yield to Christ our sins are blotted out, buried in the deepest sea. They are remembered no more (Acts 3:19 and Psalm 51:9).

Exactly When It Happened

A young man was working his way among the people in the gate area of an airport. As the people waited for the boarding announcement to be made, he was handing out copies of that little booklet *The Four Spiritual Laws*, doing a faithful work of evangelism.

There was an elderly African-American man slumped in a seat in the waiting area, sound asleep. He was a dignified figure with white curly hair and a fashionably tailored suit. This old man was as sound asleep as a man could get, but the young evangelist was not about to be deterred by that. He tapped the man on the knee. When the old man woke, he was extremely startled. He blurted out, "Where am I? What's going on? What's happening?" The persistent young man simply and sternly asked, "Sir! Are you saved?"

"Yeah," said the old man. "I guess I'm saved! I suppose I'm saved! Yes! I'm probably saved!"

"That's not good enough!" the young man responded. "Can you tell me exactly when you were saved?"

"Not exactly," the old man answered. "It was almost two thousand years ago!"

Now that's good theology. Our salvation is dependent on what Jesus did two thousand years ago. That's when our salvation was purchased and when we were delivered from the punishment for our sins. We may have just found out about it recently, but Jesus did what needed to be done long ago and far away, on an old rugged cross.

Blank Tape

When I was a young boy, an evangelist came to our church, and told us that on Judgment Day they would pull down a movie screen and run a film (or in today's terminology, a video), and flashed up on the screen would be pictures of every dirty, filthy thing we had ever done. Then, he looked at me and said, "And your mother will be there!" I shuddered at the thought!

During the Watergate hearings, prosecutors produced a cassette tape alleged to be an actual recording of Richard Nixon ordering two staff members to proceed with the cover-up of the whole Watergate affair. During the hearings they put Rosemary Woods, Nixon's private secretary, on the stand as they played the tape for all to hear. A good part of the American public watched the whole thing on live television. It was the highest kind of drama.

The tape played to the point where the crime was allegedly recorded, then suddenly the tape went dead. America watched and listened for eighteen and a half minutes while the tape played, but they heard nothing. Rosemary Woods had erased the tape!

The reason I like to tell that story at this point is to let people know that there probably isn't a videotape with all of my sins recorded on it. And there probably isn't a videotape with your sin recorded on it. But if there were, here's the good news of the gospel: JESUS HAS ERASED YOUR TAPE!

I Forgot

The story is told of a Catholic bishop who was upset because a woman in his diocese claimed to have daily conversations with Jesus. A little cult had grown up around her, and every day people surrounded her house, got on their knees, prayed, sang hymns, and said the rosary.

The bishop thought all of this was getting out of hand, so he went to visit the woman. He told her that while he knew she *thought* she was having conversations with Jesus, he was pretty much convinced it was all part of her imagination. To prove his point he said, "If Jesus is right here in this room with you now, and you can talk to Him, then ask Him to name the three sins I confessed this morning when I went to the confessional. After having what you believe to be a conversation with Jesus, if you can accurately name those sins, I might believe in what you say."

The woman sat for a long while. Then she smiled and turned to the bishop and said, "I asked Him, but Jesus said, 'I forgot.'"

We have a God who not only forgives, He forgets. He takes sin away from us and forgets it was ever ours in the first place.

The Grenade

A new recruit went into training at Paris Island, hoping to become a marine. He was one of those young men who seemed to be a bit out of step with the norm, and he easily became the subject of ridicule for those who enjoy picking on off beat people.

In the particular barracks to which this young marine was assigned, there was an extremely high level of meanness. The other young men did everything they could to make a joke of the new recruit and to humiliate him. One day, someone came up with the bright idea that they could scare the daylights out of this young marine by dropping a disarmed hand grenade onto the floor and pretending it was about to go off. Everyone else knew about this and they were all ready to get a big laugh.

The hand grenade was thrown into the middle of the floor, and the warning was yelled, "It's a live grenade, it's a live grenade! It's about to explode!"

They fully expected that the young man would get hysterical and perhaps jump out a window. Instead, the young marine fell on the grenade, hugged it to his stomach, and yelled to the other men in the barracks, "Run for your lives! Run for your lives! You'll be killed if you don't!"

The other marines froze in stillness and shame. They realized that the one they had scorned was the one ready to lay down his life for them.

And so it was with Jesus.

Timeless

According to Einstein's theory of relativity, time is relative to motion. The faster we travel, the more time is compressed. Hypothetically, if you could travel in a rocket into outer space at 170,000 miles per second, then returned in ten years, you would be ten years older, but all the rest of us would be twenty years older. Our twenty years would be compressed into ten years of your time.

If you could travel at 180,000 miles per second, our twenty years would be compressed into one day of your time. And, if you could travel at 186,000 miles per second—that's the speed of light—then all of time would be compressed into one instantaneous now. Perhaps another way of putting this is to say that everything would be simultaneous. At the speed of light, time as we know it ceases to exist.

I believe that when Jesus hung on the cross two thousand years ago, He was both man and God, as contradictory and impossible as that sounds. As a man, He died, and His death is a done deal. However, because He was also God on the cross, He was, and He is, simultaneous with every human being along the broad continuum of history. What I'm telling you is that even as you read this, Jesus at Calvary is simultaneous with you. From the cross He is looking at you right now. In His Godness, Jesus experiences time in another dimension. That's why He could say, "Before Abraham was, I AM!" He wasn't using poor grammar. He was telling us that before there was ever an Abraham, that was present tense for Him. He's also telling us that at this very moment, each of us is part of His eternal now.

As He hangs on the cross two thousand years ago, Jesus is contemporaneous with you, even as you read this. And, if you will let Him, He will reach out from the cross and connect with you. Like a sponge, He will absorb out of you the dark side of your humanity. He will drain out of you, as though His body were absorbing it by osmosis, everything that is dirty and filthy and ugly. It will be absorbed into His person! Into His being! That's why the Bible says, "He who knew no sin became sin for our sake."

Jesus Loves Me

The great Swiss-German theologian Karl Barth delivered one of the closing lectures of his life at the University of Chicago Divinity School. At the end of the lecture, the president of the seminary told the audience that Dr. Barth was not well and was very tired, and though he thought Dr. Barth would like to be open for questions, he probably could not handle the strain. Then he said, "Therefore, I'll ask just one question on behalf of all of us." He turned to Barth and asked, "Of all the theological insights you have ever had, which do you consider to be the greatest of them all?"

This was a remarkable question to ask of a man who had written tens of thousands of pages of some of the most sophisticated theology ever put on paper. The students sat with pads and pencils ready. They wanted to jot down the premier insight of the greatest theologian of their time.

Karl Barth closed his eyes and thought for a while. Then he smiled, opened his eyes, and said to the young seminarians, "The greatest theological insight that I have ever had is this: Jesus loves me, this I know, for the Bible tells me so!"

Jesus Waits to Be Met in Others

The major theme in my theology is the belief that the same Jesus who died on the cross, was resurrected, and is coming again, is also spiritually present in a personal way in our world right now. I picked up this theme from my hero for Christian living, St. Francis of Assisi.

The Leper

Francis, himself, had a strange encounter with Jesus. He was on his way to do battle for his city. He was dressed in armor, riding upon his horse down the road to Perugia. Suddenly, there was standing in his way a leper dressed in rags. A good part of the leper's face had been eaten away by the dreaded disease. Francis bade the leper to step aside, but the man just stood there, silently.

On an impulse, Francis got off his horse, went up to the leper, and gave him some money. Still, the leper did not move.

Francis then took off his cape and wrapped it around the man. Still, the leper did not move.

Finally, Francis took the man's head in his hands and kissed him on his rotted lips. When he got back on his horse and looked down to say good-bye to the leper, the road was empty. The leper was nowhere to be found, and Francis knew that in the leper he had encountered Jesus Christ.

The Least of These

All who become spiritually sensitive have had encounters such as Francis had. Maybe they're not as dramatic, but if you have the eyes to see, you will see Jesus—especially in the poor and the oppressed. I must have told the story a thousand times of being on a landing strip just outside the border of the Dominican Republic in northern Haiti. A small airplane was supposed to pick me up and fly me back to the capital city. As I stood there searching the sky for the airplane, a woman came toward me holding her child in her arms. The baby was emaciated. His arms and legs hung from his little body as though they were sticks. The child's stomach was swollen four or five times the normal size, not because he had had too much to eat, but because he had had nothing to eat at all. Digestive fluids had eaten up the insides of the child and the swelling was the inevitable result.

The woman held up her child with his rust-colored hair and shrunken face, and she began to plead with me, "Take my baby! Take my baby! Please, mister, take my baby. If you don't take my baby, my baby's going to die. Take my baby. Please, take my baby!"

I tried to tell her there was nothing I could do to help her. I tried to explain that I couldn't take her baby. I tried to look away, but no matter which direction I turned she was in my face, pleading with me to take her child. "Make my baby your baby," she kept saying. "Feed my baby. Take my baby to a hospital. Save my baby. Please! Please! Please!"

I was relieved when the little Piper Cub airplane came into sight. The minute it touched down at the end of the grass landing strip I ran across the field to meet it. But the woman came running after me screaming, "Take my baby! Take my baby! Take my baby!"

I climbed into the plane as fast as I could and closed the door. I told the pilot to rev up the engine and get us out of there. He got the engine up to speed, but not soon enough. The woman was alongside the plane, holding her dying child in one arm and banging on the door with the other. But the airplane pulled away from her and went slowly down the landing strip, then into the air.

I was halfway back to the capital when it hit me, and I realized whom I had left behind on that grass landing strip. It was Jesus! I don't really know the name of the child, but I could hear the words of Jesus, as recorded in Matthew 25:42–43, saying, "For I was an hungred, and ye gave me no meat: I was thirsty, and ye gave me no drink: I was a stranger, and ye took me not in: naked, and ye clothed me not: sick, and in prison, and ye visited me not."

I hear myself saying in return, "Lord, when saw we thee an hungred, or athirst, or a stranger, or naked, or sick, or in prison, and did not minister unto thee?"

And Jesus answers, "Inasmuch as ye did it not to one of the least of these, ye did it not to me" (Matt. 25:45).

I believe that Jesus mystically presented Himself to me through that child, and when I rejected that child, I rejected Jesus. It's good news to me that I am saved by grace and not of works. Because only by the grace of God can I be saved from such failures.

The Sacramental Poor

St. Francis told us that we must regard the poor as sacramental. He taught us to believe that if we have the eyes to see, every time we look into the eyes of the poor and the oppressed, we will have the eerie awareness that Christ is staring back at us.

Whenever I talk about the poor being sacramental the Catholics get happy, because they are into sacraments big time. They believe that in holy communion the bread literally becomes the flesh of Jesus and the wine is literally transubstantiated into His blood. At the other end of the theological spectrum are people like me. I'm Baptist. We believe that in holy communion the bread stays bread and the wine remains wine, and that the elements just symbolize the body and blood of Christ.

Between those two extremes are the Episcopalians and Lutherans. They believe that in holy communion the bread stays bread and the wine stays wine, but coming through the elements is the real presence of Christ. It is still normal bread and wine, but Christ is experienced in them.

I'm not about to affirm one theology of holy communion over another, but I do know that what the Episcopalians and Lutherans say about the bread and wine is what St. Francis taught us about the poor and the oppressed. They need not be holy and they need not be Christian, but *through* them Christ comes to us. As we love them and as we care for them, we are loving and caring for Jesus Himself. He waits to be loved in them.

I'm Jesus

During World War II, the Nazis came into a Polish village, rounded up the Jews, lined them up in front of a firing squad, and killed them. The bodies of the dead fell into a huge grave, which the Jews themselves had dug. As dirt was shoveled over the bodies, no one was aware that there was a boy being buried among the dead who had not been touched by any of the bullets. He slowly dug his way out of the grave. By the time he emerged from the dirt, night had fallen. The boy ran back into the village, hoping that some of the people there would take him in. But every door that opened was immediately shut when the people inside saw who he was. They recognized the boy. They knew he was one of the Jews who had been shot at by the firing squad. They wanted nothing to do with him, lest the Nazis punish them for harboring a Jewish child. Finally, he knocked on one door, and before it could be shut in his face, he cried out to the woman inside, "Don't you recognize me? I'm Jesus! Don't you recognize me?" The woman swept the child into the house, and from that day on cared for him as though he was one of her own.

In later life, when that boy had grown up, he always remembered that fateful evening, but he could never figure out why he said what he said. But I think I know why. I think that at such moments the Spirit of God puts words in our mouths (Exod. 4:15).

The Fat Lady

J. D. Salinger picks up the same message of Christ being among the needy in his book *Franny and Zooey.* If you've read the book, you know that Franny returns from her studies at the university emotionally and psychologically messed up. She had gotten caught up in some religious cult that had left her confused and depressed. Her brother Zooey does his best to bring her around. He finally succeeds by reminding her of something that happened in their childhood.

Their family had had a radio show in which the children functioned as super geniuses, answering any questions the interrogators would throw their way. Zooey asks Franny to remember what their older brother, Seymour, would say to them just before they went on the air. Franny remembers that Seymour always told them to shine their shoes, straighten up their clothes, and comb their hair. He told them to do the very best they could, because they were doing it for "the Fat Lady."

Zooey says, "This terribly clear, clear picture of the Fat Lady formed in my mind. I had her sitting on this porch all day, swatting flies, with her radio going full-blast from morning till night. I figured the heat was terrible, and she probably had cancer, and—I don't know. Anyway, it seemed . . . clear why Seymour wanted me to shine my shoes when I went on the air. It made *sense*."

Then Franny gives the image that came to her mind. "I had her in an *awful* wicker chair. She had cancer, *too*, though, and she had the radio going full-blast all day! Mine did, too!"

Then Zooey goes on to say, "But I'll tell you a terrible secret—*There isn't anyone out there who isn't Seymour's Fat Lady.* That includes your Professor Tupper, buddy. And all his . . . cousins by the dozens. There isn't anyone *anywhere* that isn't Seymour's Fat Lady."[1]

Meeting Jesus

The pastor of a large inner-city congregation established a soup kitchen in the basement of his church to help feed the many derelicts and homeless people who hung around that part of the city. These needy folk flocked to the church day in and day out to get the help they needed to survive.

Over time, these derelict and homeless people began to wander into the eleven o'clock Sunday worship service at the church. The upper-middle-class folks who worshiped at that time felt uncomfortable with such lower-class visitors. Eventually, one of the church leaders took the pastor aside and asked him, "Do these people have to be here with us? Can't we provide a special service just for them?"

The pastor answered, "Well, I think everybody should have a chance to meet Jesus face to face."

"Of course," said the deacon, "everybody should have a chance to meet Jesus. I think they should have the same opportunities to meet Jesus face to face as we all do."

The pastor shot back, "I'm not talking about them! I'm talking about you!"

I'm sure that gave the deacon a lot to think about. The pastor

↶ A friend of mine was taking a tour of an inner-city church with a huge social ministry that included a soup kitchen. He was there just before the noon hour. The kitchen crew had gathered in a huddle to pray before they opened the door and let in the hungry street people. Among the prayers lifted up was one by an elderly African-American woman who simply said, "Lord, we know You'll be comin' through the line today, so help us to treat You well!"

had made it clear that what he really needed was to encounter Jesus in the homeless people who wandered into that church Sunday after Sunday. Such encounters sanctify us.

Sharing Coffee

If you need some good stories, just come to Philadelphia and wander around the streets downtown. You will meet many wonderful people and have many varied experiences. You will certainly come away enriched by some strange encounters.

One day, about the noon hour, I was walking down Chestnut Street when I noticed a bum walking toward me. He was covered with dirt and soot from head to toe. There was filthy stuff caked on his skin. But the most noticeable thing about him was his beard. It hung down almost to his waist and there was rotted food stuck in it. The man was holding a cup of McDonald's coffee and the lip of the cup was already smudged from his dirty mouth. As he staggered toward me, he seemed to be staring into his cup of coffee. Then, suddenly, he looked up and he yelled, "Hey, mister! Ya want some of my coffee?"

I have to admit that I really didn't. But I knew that the right thing to do was to accept his generosity, and so I said, "I'll take a sip."

As I handed the cup back to him I said, "You're getting pretty generous, aren't you, giving away your coffee? What's gotten into you today that's made you so generous?"

The old derelict looked straight into my eyes and said, "Well . . . the coffee was especially delicious today, and I figure if God gives you something good, you ought to share it with people!"

I thought to myself, *Oh, man. He has really set me up. This is going to cost me five dollars.* I asked him, "I suppose there's something I can do for you in return, isn't there?"

The bum answered, "Yeah! You can give me a hug!" (To tell the truth, I was hoping for the five dollars.)

He put his arms around me and I put my arms around him. Then suddenly I realized something. He wasn't going to let me go! People were passing us on the sidewalk. They were staring at me. There I was, dressed in establishment garb, hugging this dirty, filthy bum! I was embarrassed. I didn't know what to do. Then, little by little, my embarrassment changed to awe and reverence. I heard a voice echoing down the corridors of time saying "I was hungry; did you feed Me? I was naked; did you clothe Me? I was sick; did you care for Me? I was the bum you met on Chestnut Street . . . did you hug Me? For if you did it to the least of these, you did it unto Me."

Go to Jesus

Will Campbell at one time handled civil rights issues as an employee of the National Council of Churches, but he is now a self-appointed missionary to "rednecks." I heard him preach a sermon once, critiquing "the invitation" as it is given in most Baptist churches. Those of us who are acquainted with such invitations know that at the end of a sermon, the preacher of a good evangelical congregation invites people who want to commit their lives to Christ to come down the aisle to indicate that desire.

Will said, "I hope that someday there will be an evangelistic service in which, when the preacher gives the invitation and people start coming down the aisle, he yells back at them, 'Don't come down the aisle! Go to Jesus! Don't come to me! Go to Jesus!'

"Upon that declaration, the people who were coming down the aisle turn around and exit the auditorium and get in their cars and drive away. He then yells at the rest of the congregation, 'Why are you hanging around here? Why don't you go to Jesus too? Why don't you all go to Jesus?' The people rise en masse and quickly leave the church, and soon the parking lot is empty.

"What I imagine is that about a half hour later the telephone at the police station starts ringing off the hook, and the voice at the other end says, 'We're down here at the old-folks' home and there's some crazy people at the door yelling that they want to come in and visit Jesus, and I keep telling them Jesus isn't in here! All we have in here is a bunch of old ladies who are half dead. But they keep saying, "But we want to visit Jesus! We want to visit Jesus!"'

"The next call is from the warden down at the prison. He's saying, 'Send some cops down here! There's a bunch of nuts at the gate and they're yelling and screaming, "Let us in there! We want to visit Jesus! We want to visit Jesus!" I keep telling them that all we have in this place are murderers, rapists, and thieves. But they keep yelling, "Let us in! We want to visit Jesus!"'

"No sooner does the cop at the desk hang up the phone than it rings again. This time it's the superintendent of the state hospital calling for help. He's complaining that there are a bunch of weird people outside begging to be let in. They, too, want to see Jesus! The superintendent says, 'I keep telling them Jesus isn't here. All we have here are a bunch of nuts, but they keep yelling at us, "We want to see Jesus."'"

I love to tell Will's story because it illustrates, in a brilliant way, that to go to Jesus is to go to those who are the rejects of society. We encounter Him there.

3

What We Overhear about the Holy Spirit

Whenever I think about the work of the Holy Spirit, I immediately think about what my friends in the Vineyard churches call "signs and wonders." Indeed, there are signs and wonders all around us, and more things are happening that ought to be called miraculous than we are ready to affirm.

The Power of Miracles

The Flat Tire

I, myself, can attest to one miracle that defies any talk of natural explanation. When I was in high school, our family was very, very poor. I took a number of odd jobs trying to help out my parents.

One day, I discovered there was a large bakery just a few blocks from our house that at the end of the day made bread available for sale at one-tenth the regular price. I quickly figured out that there were a couple of diners around who would buy that bread from me at triple the price I paid for it. And so I became an entrepreneur. At nine o'clock at night I would go to the bakery, buy a pile of bread, put it in a wagon that was tied to the rear of my bike, deliver it to the diners, and sell it.

The miracle happened one night after I had delivered all the bread and was on my way home. By then, it was about eleven o'clock. There was a freezing drizzle in the air that soaked my coat and made my body shiver. I don't remember a night being any darker or colder than that one seemed to be, and as I tried to make my way home I felt nothing but misery. Then, all of a sudden, the tire of my bicycle blew out. I had one of those old Schwinn bikes with balloon tires, and when a tire blew it did it with a bang. It's hard to describe what I thought and felt at that moment. I got off my bike, sat down on the curb, put my head in my hands, and started to cry. I was tired and I was beaten. I had tried so hard to be a good boy and earn some money for my family, and then this had to happen. I remember moaning, "God, everybody thinks You're good, and maybe You are to other people, but it seems like You're mean to me. How could You let this happen? Why can't You help me? You know what? I think after today, I'm just not going to believe in You anymore!"

I don't know how long I sat there, but eventually I got up and started to push my bicycle on what I knew would be a long trek home in the freezing rain. I hadn't gone very far when I noticed a gasoline station. I don't know what made me do it, but I went over to the air pump in the station and tried to put some air in the blown-out tire. Usually those pumps are turned off at the end of the day, and there was no air to be had when the compressor wasn't working. If I had stopped to think about it, I would have known how futile it was to try to put air in that tire. It was blown out—bad! But I tried. I put the nozzle from the air pump onto the valve of my tire and pulled the lever that releases the air. Incredibly, air flowed! The tire inflated! I couldn't believe it.

I didn't hesitate. I climbed on my bike and pedaled home in the dark, saying over and over again, "Thank You, Jesus! Thank You, Jesus! Thank You, Jesus!"

When I got to my house, I carried my bicycle up onto the front porch and locked it up. It was then about eleven-thirty. I put the key into the lock of the front door, and just as I was about to turn it, there was a sudden swishing sound. I turned around and watched as all the air left the tire. Within seconds, the blown-out tire was completely flat again.

In the morning, when I went to look at the tire, I saw there was a rip on the side of it that was at least three inches long. The inner tube was torn apart. I knew that something miraculous had happened!

Looking back on that evening, I honestly believe that God looked down and saw a kid who had been pushed just as far as he could go. I was on the edge and He wasn't willing to allow me to be pushed beyond that which I was able to bear. The Bible promises that God intervenes in such situations (1 Cor. 10:13). I have a feeling that I just might have given up on the whole Christian thing if God hadn't stepped in with a miracle at that point. But He did!

Not Cured, Healed

A couple of years ago I was at a church conference in South Africa. The other speaker was one of the founders of the movement often referred to as the Toronto Blessing. This is a movement that very much believes in a theology of signs and wonders. Those engaged in this ministry contend that miracles are part of the witness that we should have to an unbelieving world as we try to win people to Christ.

This particular evangelist was very respectful of me, even though miracles were not any part of my ministry. When he asked if I was into healing people, I explained to him that when I'm with people who are sick, I always pray for them to be healed, but to be perfectly honest, I hadn't ever seen anything spectacular happen. My friend jokingly reminded me that not seeing anything spectacular happen hadn't deterred me from being a preacher. We both laughed, even as he affirmed that the ministry of Christ was to preach, to teach, and to heal, and that all three of those things should be part of what we do in our everyday service for the Kingdom.

The next week I was back in the States and preaching at a church in Oregon. On impulse, as I ended the service I said to the congregation that if anyone wanted to remain behind for healing, I would be glad to pray with them. I told them they shouldn't expect much to happen, because nothing much happens when I pray, but if they wanted to give it a try, I'd be willing to pray as hard as I could. Surprisingly, about thirty people stayed behind and waited patiently as I prayed for one after the other.

I did not want to do this healing thing fast, like some of the healers I see on television. I wanted to really talk to a person before I prayed and get a feel for what was on that person's heart. I wanted to hug each person and connect with him or her as deeply as I knew how. I did that with each of the people who stayed behind, and in each case I put some olive oil that I had brought along with me on each of their heads. It took me more than an hour to pray through that little group. But I did it! What intrigued me was that most of the people who had come for healing had nothing physically wrong with them. One man needed healing for an addiction to pornography. One woman wanted healing for her marriage. Someone else asked healing for anger. But there were a few who did have physical illnesses.

Four days later I got a telephone call, and the woman at the other end said, "Tony, on Sunday you prayed for my husband. He had cancer."

When I heard the word "had" my heart quickened a bit. *"Had* cancer?" I asked.

The woman answered, "Well, he's dead now."

When she said that I thought to myself, *A lot of good I do.*

Then the woman said, "You don't understand. When my husband and I walked into that church on Sunday, he was angry with God. He had cancer and he knew he was going to be dead soon, and he hated God for letting it happen. He wanted to see his grandchildren grow up more than anything. At night he would lie in bed and curse God. It was horrible. And the angrier he got toward God, the meaner he was to everyone around him. It was unbearable to be in the same room with him. His nastiness just kept getting worse and worse and worse. But then you laid hands on him on Sunday morning and you prayed for him. When he walked out of church I knew there was something different. I could feel it. He was a different person. The last four days of our lives have been the best four days we've ever had together. We talked and laughed. We even sang hymns with each other. It was a good, good time."

She paused, then added something really profound. She said, "Tony, he wasn't cured, but he was healed."

I hung up the phone, knowing I had learned something about the work of the Holy Spirit.

The Duck Lady

Another miracle I want to tell you about took place one evening following a lecture I gave at the University of Pennsylvania. I was standing at the corner of 34th and Spruce Streets when I heard the Duck Lady coming. We called her the Duck Lady because this schizophrenic homeless bag woman never stopped making quacking sounds. You could hear her coming a long way off, because she was really loud at it. I could hear her that evening with her "Quack! Quack! Quack! Quack!" She came right alongside me.

As I waited for the light to change, for some reason I didn't understand, I turned slowly toward her. Strangely enough, she simultaneously turned toward me. Our eyes met, and there was a mystical encounter! The dynamism of the Holy Spirit enabled me to look not *at* her, but *into* her. With an energy that flowed from within, I reached through her eyes and down into the depths of her being. With all the power of the Spirit that was in me, I reached out to her and into her soul.

Jesus once said that the light of the body is the eye (Matt. 6:22). I think it is better translated as "the eyes are the entrance to the body," because if people shut off their eyes, as Jesus said, then they are in darkness. The Duck Lady's eyes were the entrance to her soul, and the Spirit in me connected with her soul as I stared into her eyes.

She stopped her quacking! I had never known her to stop quacking before. But she stopped! Then her face lit up in an expression of awe and wonder. She looked around, and as though in a trance, she said, "It's beautiful! It's really beautiful!" She gasped as she took in the trees and the sky around her.

Before I could respond, the traffic light changed. Someone bumped against her and I watched her head shake. Then she fell back into her schizophrenic state, and she started quacking again. She wandered down the sidewalk aimlessly and disappeared amidst the other people on the street.

As I stood there processing it all, I thought to myself, *If only I could have held on to her a little longer. If only I could have loved her a little more. If only we could have stayed connected in the Holy Spirit for just a few more minutes, perhaps the deliverance would not have been momentary. Perhaps it would have been lasting.*

There are those who would say, "You're supposed to be a social scientist. Don't you think the Duck Lady was a case to be handled by psychiatrists and psychotherapists?"

To such a question I can only answer, "But of course!" The psychotherapist and the psychiatrist should have a chance at her, but after they have done all they can, and still yield no healing, I am ready to declare that "There is a balm in Gilead that heals the sin-sick soul."

Oops!

There are so many wonderful things happening under the auspices of the Pentecostal and charismatic movements, that even an old Baptist like me has to admit there's something authentic going on out there among them. However, wherever there are true things going on in the name of Jesus, there are likely to be phony ones. There will always be people who pretend to have spiritual powers and experiences when they really don't.

A friend of mine told me about being in a meeting in a charismatic church where a woman stood up in the middle of the service. She claimed to have a word of prophecy. She stood in a trancelike state, and when she spoke an unnatural, heavy voice came out of her. Everyone waited with intense anticipation as she said boldly, "Thus saith the Lord . . . even as Moses led the animals into the ark, even so shall I lead My people to safety, if they trust in Me."

Throughout the congregation people leaned over to one another and whispered, "Did she say *Moses?* I think she said *Moses!*"

After delivering what was supposed to be a direct message from the Lord, the woman sat down. Then, a couple of minutes later she stood up again. And again, supposedly still in a trance, she belted out, "Thus saith the Lord . . . it wasn't *Moses*, it was *Noah!*"

There were muffled giggles all over the place. Obviously there was something amiss in all of this.

The Fruits of the Spirit

I am absolutely convinced that the gifts of the Holy Spirit are for our present times. I believe that people who surrender to God and allow the Holy Spirit to take possession of them end up exercising gifts such as those that were evident in the life of the New Testament Church. There are some with gifts of preaching, others with the gift of teaching, and still others with the gift of healing. I could go on and on listing all the various *gifts* of the Spirit as outlined in Scripture. However, I am convinced that the gifts of the Spirit are not what is of ultimate significance. As important as they are in the life of the church, it seems clear to me that more important than the gifts of the Spirit are the *fruits* of the Spirit. We can see them listed in Galatians the fifth chapter: "But the fruit of the Spirit is love, joy, peace, longsuffering, gentleness, goodness, faith, meekness, temperance." It seems to me that while it is wonderful to exercise one of the gifts, having the fruits of the Spirit is far more important. The apostle Paul makes this point in 1 Corinthians 13. He tells us that we can speak with the tongues of men and of angels, but if we don't have love (which is the first and foremost fruit of the Spirit), then we are nothing. To those who exercise the gift of prophecy Paul gives great affirmation. And he does the same for those who have "a word of knowledge from the Lord." But Paul goes on in this great "love chapter" to say that one can exercise the gift of prophecy and have a word of knowledge, but without love such gifts are worthless. Therefore, the rest of this chapter will be about the ultimate fruit of the Spirit, love.

Father Kolbe

Several years ago I had the opportunity to visit Auschwitz, that horrendous Nazi prison camp. To go to that place is a horrific experience. It's not what you see, but what you feel that affects you. Something ugly lingers. Vicious hatred and sadness seem to be in the very air you breathe. Beyond all of that, there is a permeating sense of evil. Of all the things that struck me as I toured that demonic place, I was perhaps most moved by this one large room where there was a huge pile of children's shoes. I couldn't help but think of all the children who had once worn them, and how their lives had been destroyed by the diabolical anti-Semitism of the Nazis. But, there was one thing the tour guide showed me that lifted my spirits. It was the cell of a Roman Catholic priest, Father Maximilian Kolbe. He had done something magnificent with his life, even in that terrible place. He had been a blessing in a place that was cursed.

The Nazi captors had an ugly way of deterring prisoners from trying to escape. If ever someone did escape, all the remaining prisoners were lined up and six were chosen at random to be hung. Nevertheless, there were escapes. After one escape, the six men picked for death stood on the scaffold with ropes around their necks, when something incredible happened. Before the trapdoors could be opened and their bodies hung, Father Kolbe asked to be heard. He pled with the commandant to let him take the place of one of the men who were about to die. Pointing to one particular man, Franciszek Gajowniczek, he said, "He's from my village. I know him. He's a good man and he has a wife and several children. On the other hand, I am a priest. I am not married and I have no children at all. I do not have a family that needs me. Let me be hung in his place!"

The commandant acceded to this startling request and Father Kolbe took the place of the designated man on the gallows, and a few moments later was dead. This was love in action. And, as has been said over and over again, there is no greater love than the love that would cause one person to lay down his life for another.

When I visited the cell that had once held Father Kolbe, the tour guide pointed out a vase that contained fresh flowers. She explained that when the war was over the man who had been saved by Father Kolbe's sacrifice moved his family to the town of Auschwitz so that they could regularly come to the cell and place flowers there, to revere the man who had sacrificed so much for them.

He Went Higher

In the Hasidic Jewish tradition there is the story of a rabbi who was so holy that it was rumored that on Sabbath afternoons he ascended into heaven to personally commune with God. One day, a couple of boys from the synagogue decided to follow the rabbi after Sabbath services to see whether he did, indeed, ascend to heaven. What they saw instead was that the rabbi spent the afternoon going to the homes of elderly and sick gentile people. He cooked meals for old ladies and cleaned the houses of old men.

On the next Sabbath some of the elders jokingly asked the boys whether the rabbi had really ascended to heaven to commune with God. The boys answered, "Oh, no, he did not ascend into heaven. He went much higher!"

The Janitor

We all have a tendency to equate the work of the Holy Spirit with dramatic events. But the work of the Holy Spirit isn't always spectacular. I love the old hymn that says, "For not with swords loud clashing, Nor roll of stirring drums, With deeds of love and mercy, The heavenly Kingdom comes." It's often in an array of little things that the work of the Spirit is expressed.

But it may also be said that evidence of the *lack* of spirituality is found in behavior that metes out thoughtless acts that hurt others, with no guilt being felt. For instance, I went into the men's room at the Amtrak station in Philadelphia once, and to my surprise, I saw working there one of the dear men from my church. He was the one who cleaned the floors, washed out the toilets, and maintained the cleanliness of the place. When I asked him about his job, he told me it was okay, and that it really didn't bother him to work there. The only thing that really bothered him, he told me, was when he had to pick the cigarette butts out of the urinals. I can still hear him ask me, "When those smokers throw their cigarette butts in the urinals, don't they realize that somebody's got to go in there and dig them out? Don't they even think about what it's like to reach in there and pull out those soggy cigarette butts, and throw them in a plastic bag? Don't people ever think about other people?"

Good question!

She Can Have Mine!

A schoolteacher served students from several grades in a small one-room schoolhouse in upstate New York, including one child who was euphemistically referred to as "special." That particular little boy was what we might call "slow."

When Christmas came, the teacher decided to put on a Christmas pageant, and the slow boy wanted to have a part in it. He didn't want to just stand around on the stage; he wanted to have a speaking part. They all knew that he could not remember lines very well, but they came up with what seemed like a viable solution to the problem. They told him that he could be the innkeeper. When Mary and Joseph knocked at the door of the inn, he was to open it and say, "No room!" Mary would then say something, and when she finished her lines he was to say again, "No room!" They thought he could handle this, but just to make sure, they appointed someone to stand near him and poke him at the proper time and whisper the right words in his ear, should he forget them.

The night of the Christmas pageant all seemed to be going well until Mary and Joseph got to the inn door. Mary knocked. When our little friend opened the door he said what was expected of him: "No room!" Mary responded, "But, sir, it's cold. Have you no place at all where we can stay? It's freezing and I'm sick. I'm going to have a baby, and unless you help us, my baby will be born in the cold, cold night." The boy just stood there and said nothing. The prompter nudged him and whispered, "No room! Say, 'No room!'"

The boy turned to the prompter and blurted out, "I know what I'm supposed to say! But she can have my room!"

To some, loving comes easily and almost without thinking. The rest of us must be more deliberate, and it is to that end that the Holy Spirit comes.

The Wrong One

One afternoon, as I sat in my office, the telephone rang. It was my mother. She told me that Mrs. Kirkpatrick had died and that the least I could do was to go to the funeral. My mother, like all Italians, was big on funerals. She felt that it was of enormous importance to show "respect" and honor the deceased with our presence. So, while I was growing up I attended more funerals than I can remember out of "respect." However, in Mrs. Kirkpatrick's case, it was more than respect that made me say yes to my mother's request. Mrs. Kirkpatrick was a lovely lady, and as we were growing up she did many wonderful things for the children of our church. I could always count on her giving me candy at Christmastime. On one occasion she took me to a concert so that I could hear a symphony orchestra play. Mrs. Kirkpatrick had added much to my life, and my mother was right. Going to her funeral was the least I could do to show respect and appreciation.

I arrived at the funeral home at two o'clock, just as the funeral was scheduled to begin. I rushed up the steps and hurried by the somber man at the door. There were several funerals in progress at the time. I walked into what I thought was the designated room for Mrs. Kirkpatrick's funeral and quickly took a seat. I had done it so hurriedly, I failed to notice that, other than an elderly woman sitting two seats away from me, there was no one else in the entire room. I looked over the edge of the casket and *he* did not look like Mrs. Kirkpatrick! I had the wrong funeral! I was just about to leave when the woman reached over and grabbed me by the arm, and with desperation in her voice said, "You *were* his friend—weren't you?"

I didn't know what to say. Dietrich Bonhoeffer, the famous German martyr, once said, "There comes a time in every man's life when he must lie with imagination, with vigor and with enthusiasm!" I don't know whether you concur with Bonhoeffer, but just for the record, you should know that I lied. What else could I do? The woman was reaching out for assurance that somebody had some connection with her husband and some concern for her. What was I to say? "I'm sorry, I'm at the wrong funeral. Your husband didn't have any friends." She needed to know that there was somebody to whom her husband meant something. And so I lied and said I knew him, and that he was always kind to me.

I went through the funeral sitting at her side. Afterward, the two of us went out and got into the sole automobile that would follow the hearse to the cemetery. I figured that since I had gone that far, I might as well go all the way. I wasn't about to leave this poor old lady alone in her hour of deep sadness.

We stood at the edge of the grave and said some prayers. As the casket was lowered into the grave, each of us threw a flower onto it. We then got back into the car and returned to the funeral home. As we arrived there, I took this elderly woman's hand and said to her, "Mrs. King, I have to tell you something. I really did not know your husband. I want to be your friend, and I can't be your friend after today unless I tell you the truth. I did not know your husband. I came to the funeral by mistake."

I waited a long while wondering how she would respond. She took my hand and held it for what seemed an interminable moment, then answered, "You'll never ever, ever know how much your being with me meant to me today."

I know there will be those who will say I should never have lied to this woman in the first place. But then, they weren't there. I had a feeling at the end of that day that there was a voice within me, speaking to me and saying, "Well done, thou good and faithful servant!"

By Our Love

The love generated by the Holy Spirit extends not only to people we know, but even to people we don't. This was made very clear to me some years ago when I was the speaker for an evangelistic crusade held at the Arco Arena in Sacramento, California. The first night of the evangelistic crusade was a brilliant success. Thousands of people came to the meeting. There was good music and the Spirit of God moved among people, leading many of them to make decisions for Christ.

The following morning there was a meeting of the planning committee. I was surprised when I realized they were upset. Not with me or anything I had done; they were upset with the media. They complained about the fact that even though thousands of people had come to hear the Word of God the night before, the television stations and newspapers paid no attention to what was going on. I listened for a while, then gave them my opinion. I pointed out that Mick Jagger had been there the previous week, filled every seat in the place, and had gotten no media coverage. It wasn't any big deal to the media, I explained, to fill a stadium or arena with thousands and thousands of people. Then I made a suggestion. "This is World AIDS Week. Let's do something about that. If you want news coverage, just put out a press release that the offering from tonight's meeting will go to programs throughout the Sacramento area that minister to people suffering from AIDS. If you want news coverage, you've got to make news! I want to tell you it's *news* when a bunch of evangelicals are willing to express love in a tangible way for people suffering from AIDS. We say we love those people, but it's usually a lot of words. Let's put our money where our mouths are and see what happens."

This was several years back, when the fear of AIDS was at a fevered pitch and contempt for those who had this dreaded disease was omnipresent. Radio preachers constantly told the Christian community that AIDS was sent by God to punish homosexuals. The rhetoric about people with AIDS was absolutely horrible. However, the people running this crusade were godly folks and thought that even apart from any news coverage we might get, such an offering would be a good thing. After all, they reflected, the bills for running the arena had been paid, and most of the other expenses had already been covered.

That night the media coverage was extensive. All three major television stations were there with camera crews, and the two newspapers were represented by reporters.

The mass choir sang, but the television cameras were not turned on. I preached, and they paid no attention. They were waiting for the offering at the end of the service. As the buckets were passed to collect the contributions that would go for people with AIDS, television cameras were turned on and newspaper photographers were snapping pictures. This was what they wanted to see. Evangelicals sacrificially giving to meet the needs of people with AIDS, most of whom at that time were homosexuals.

Later that night, I was in my hotel room watching the evening news to see how the whole thing was covered. They not only showed the offering being taken, but they interviewed people as they were leaving the arena. One old grandmother was moved to tears as she said, "My grandson has AIDS, and this is the first time that I've been able to talk about it, because up until now I was made to feel so ashamed of him. I feel he was affirmed tonight." There were a few other comments that were made, but the best one of the evening was from a tough-looking guy who was grossly overweight. His hair was a mess and it looked as though he needed a shave, but they stuck a microphone under his mouth and asked him, "Well, what did you think of the offering tonight?" The guy answered in a gruff voice, "What about it?" The interviewer said, "Well, people with AIDS are usually homosexuals, and you evangelical Christians haven't been very kindly disposed to them, have you? How do you feel about your money going to people who are probably gay?"

The guy's answer was splendid. He said, "I don't know anything about this homo stuff. All I know is that when people are sick, we're supposed to take care of them. And that's because Christians love everybody."

I stood up in the hotel room, shot my fists into the air, and yelled, "YES!"

In the end, they will know that we are Christians, not because we perform miracles, or demonstrate signs and wonders. They will know we are Christians by our love.

Party in Room 210

I head up an organization that has created a missionary enterprise in Haiti. Presently, through the efforts of those who have taken over this ministry, a network of some eighty-five schools has been established that serves children who have been reduced to a life that is pretty close to slavery. The children in these schools, for the most part, come from families that are so poor they have had to give their children away to other families who can feed them. These oppressed youngsters are given the most menial tasks imaginable, and they can expect to spend their lives in hard labor. Such children carry water for most of the day and, in between, work in the sugar fields. Classes are held from the late afternoon into the evening because these children are not free to go to school during the regular daytime hours. Nevertheless, they attend the school with great faithfulness, because they know that if they can learn to read and write, in a country where the illiteracy rate is 85 percent, they have a chance to escape their oppressive lives.

When I go down there I usually stay at a Holiday Inn right in the center of Port-au-Prince. Once, when I was walking to the entrance of the hotel, I was intercepted by three girls. I call them girls because they looked to be about fifteen or sixteen years of age. The one in the middle said, "Mister, for ten dollars you can have me all night long." I was stunned by what she had said. I turned to the girl next to her and asked, "Can I have you for ten dollars?" She nodded approval.

I asked the third girl the same question. She tried to conceal her contempt for me with a smile. But it's hard to look sexy when you're fifteen or sixteen and you're very poor and your family is hungry.

I said, "Fine! I've got thirty dollars! I'm in Room 210. You be up there in a half hour. I'll pay you then and I want all three of you for the whole night!"

I rushed up to the room and got on the phone, and called down to the concierge desk. I said, "Send every Walt Disney cartoon video you have up to Room 210. Anything by Disney. Send it up to me."

I called down to the restaurant and asked if they made banana splits. I told them that I wanted banana splits with extra everything. I wanted them to be huge and delicious. I wanted extra whipped cream, extra chocolate syrup, extra nuts. I wanted . . . I wanted . . . *four* of them!

Within the half hour the videos came, the three girls came, and the banana splits came. I sat the girls down on the edge of the bed. We ate the banana splits. We watched the videos. We had a little party as we watched the videos until about one in the morning. That's when the last of them fell asleep across the bed.

As I sat there in the stuffed chair looking at their little bodies strewn across the bed, I thought to myself, *Nothing's changed! Nothing's changed! Tomorrow they will be back on the streets. Tomorrow they will be selling their little bodies for ten dollars a throw, because there will always be rotten ugly men who will destroy the dignity of little girls for ten dollars a night. Nothing's changed!*

Then the Spirit spoke to me and said, "But, for one night, Tony, you let them be little girls again. For one night, you let them be kids. You didn't change their lives, but for one night you gave them back their childhoods."

I am convinced that that little expression of love and that little party in Room 210 of the Holiday Inn in Port-au-Prince was the work of the Holy Spirit.

Roger

Some of my friends go hard on me these days because they think I call for compassion for gay and lesbian people more than I should. They say, "It's okay to be considerate toward these folks, but you seem to be running a hobbyhorse on this issue. It seems to come up time and time again when you speak."

They complain because they do not understand that I'm trying to make up for an incredible failure during my high-school days. There was a boy in our high school named Roger. He was gay. We knew about it. We spread the word on him, and we made his life miserable. When we passed him in the hall, we would call out his name in an effeminate manner. We gestured with our hands and made him the brunt of a lot of cheap jokes. On Fridays after phys ed class, we would go into the showers, but Roger never went in with us. He was afraid to, and for good reason. When we came out of the showers we would take our wet towels and whip them at his little naked body. We thought that was a fun thing to do.

I wasn't there the day they took Roger, dragged him into the shower room, and shoved him into the corner. Folded up in a fetal position, in the corner of that tile room, he cried as five guys urinated all over him.

That night Roger went home and he went to bed sometime around ten o'clock. They said it was about two o'clock the next morning when he got up and went down to the basement of his house—and hung himself. When they told me, I realized I wasn't a Christian. Oh, I believed all the right stuff. I was as theologically sound as any evangelical could expect to be. I knew what I was sup-posed to believe and I believed it intensely, but I hadn't surrendered to the Holy Spirit. I had not yet yielded myself and allowed God's Spirit to invade me and transform me into the kind of person I ought to be. If the Holy Spirit had been in me, I would have stood up for Roger. When the guys came to make fun of him, I would have put one arm around Roger's shoulders and waved the guys off with the other and said, "Leave him alone. He's my friend. Don't mess with him." But I was afraid to be his friend. I was afraid to stand up for Roger, because I knew that if you stand up for somebody like Roger, people will begin to say nasty things about you too. And so I kept my distance, and I failed to be the loving person that Christ wanted me to be. The work of the Holy Spirit was not evident in my life. If it had been, Roger might be alive today.

4

Overhearing More Things about the Work of the Spirit

One of the most prevalent problems in the stressed world in which we live is depression. Any Christian congregation is filled with people who have a diffused sense of unhappiness that at times can be unbearable. I do not want to suggest that being in right relationship with God and being yielded to the Holy Spirit is certain to alleviate depression, especially if that depression is caused by a chemical imbalance. The causal factors for such imbalances are not always easy to discern: It could be hormonal changes, sometimes our diets are the cause, and some chemical imbalances may be genetically triggered. All of that to say, spirituality may not be a cure-all for depression. Some of the greatest saints in history suffered from bouts of depression. But having said this, I have to contend that, over all, those who have experienced the fullness of God's Spirit in their lives give ample testimony that whatever one's state may be, the Holy Spirit lifts us up to higher ground.

Joy in the Spirit

Higher Down

For several years I was involved in developing missionary work in the Dominican Republic. Traveling to some of the more remote villages of that country could really shake up a guy. The roads were full of holes and ruts. As you traveled along, you found yourself bouncing up and down, up and down, up and down, up and down in the seat

of the car. Some of our work was located in villages high in the mountains. If you wanted to visit these villages you had to travel up wind-
ing mountain roads to get to them. But even at those higher levels,
the roads were just as bad. You still bounced up and down, and up
and down in the automobile. But here's the point: When you are up
some five thousand feet above sea level, bouncing up and down, you
discover that even when you are down, you are higher than you used
to be when you were up when you were down.

All of this to say that in the Spirit you will still have down times.
But personally, I would not trade the down times I have, now that I
have been raised up by the Spirit, for the up times I had before the
Spirit flowed into my life.

Peggy Lee

For so many people in this world there is a constant malaise to life.
Many suffer from what has been called "Peggy Lee Syndrome." Older
readers will remember Peggy Lee and one of the songs that made her
famous, "Is That All There Is?" Many people feel that life was supposed to turn out to be more fulfilling, and they are disappointed.

Lord Chesterton once wrote, "There comes a time in the late
afternoon, when the children tire of their games. It is then that they
turn to torturing the cat!" We live in a world where so many people
tire of the games they play. And in their boredom and emptiness they
turn to destructive behavior. I'm sure that's the cause for a good portion of the extramarital affairs that are ruining our families. A cure for
such a malady can be found by entering into the aliveness that comes
from yielding to an infusion of the Holy Spirit.

New Trains

The ecstasy of spirituality might be compared to an experience I had
when I was seven years old. It was Christmas, and I wanted more than
anything to have a set of Lionel electric trains. I had asked my parents,

but they told me I had to ask Santa Claus. I was already skeptical about the reality of that red-flanneled saint, but I knew how the system worked. So, on a carefully picked Saturday, I went with my mother to Gimbel's department store—where the *real* one was. (I was always confused about the many Santa Clauses that appeared on the streets at Christmas time, so my mother explained to me that the others were Santa's helpers, but the real one was at Gimbel Brothers.)

As I stood in front of Santa that particular day, I shouted loud and clear, "I want electric trains!" I said it loud enough for my mother to hear. For that matter, I think half of Gimbel's heard me.

Christmas morning I tumbled down the steps and ran over to the pile of presents underneath the tree. I picked up the biggest box, tore away the paper, lifted the lid and found . . . underwear and clothes from my Aunt Madeline! I'm a pacifist, but I believe that anyone who gives a seven-year-old boy clothes for Christmas should be shot!

I went through the rest of the presents in halfhearted fashion, convinced that my hopes would not be realized. But then after a while I noticed a large box, way behind the back of the Christmas tree. And when I pulled it out the label said "for Tony." I tore open the paper, lifted the lid, and there they were—the Lionel trains I had dreamed about! I picked up the engine and hugged it to my little chest. I loved everybody. My joy knew no bounds. I loved my mother, I loved my father . . . I even loved my *sisters.*

My ecstasy lasted for about three hours, and then something happened. It wasn't that I broke the trains. Broken trains could be fixed. Something worse happened to them. They got old! In just three hours they lost the luster of newness. Once they became old, all the king's horses and all the king's men could not restore their luster again. I started to think, *You can't do much with electric trains anyway. You put them on the track, turn on the switch of the transformer, and they go around in a circle. You watch them, and watch them, and watch them, and that's it.* The joy was gone.

The Bible says that if anyone be in Christ old things pass away and all things become new (2 Cor. 5:17). The God of Scripture promises to make everything new. Our God creates an aliveness that can drive away the blues, and maintain a sense of newness about the wonders of our world that lasts a lot longer than three hours.

Fire and Joy

Blaise Pascal was considered by Albert Einstein to be the greatest intellect of the last thousand years. Pascal's contributions to mathematics, philosophy, and science were unparalleled. But perhaps his greatest contributions were in the field of religious thought. His insights in the *Pensees* laid the groundwork for the Christian version of existentialism. This seventeenth-century intellectual writes:

> FIRE! God of Abraham, God of Isaac, God of Jacob, not the god of the philosophers and the scholars—absolute certainty—beyond reason.
>
> JOY! PEACE! Forgetfulness of the world and everything, but God! The world has not known Thee, but I have known Thee. JOY! JOY! JOY! Tears of joy!

What better testimony of the joy of the Spirit than this?

Boots or No Boots

My pastor, Dr. Albert Campbell of the Mt. Carmel Baptist Church, once told this story that he set back in the days before emancipation. In those days, white folks had their seats on the main floor of the church, while African-American people were assigned seats in the balcony. There was one man named Frank, who constantly disrupted the services by shouting words of praise to God whenever the preacher said something that seemed extra good to him. Frank's white master was irritated by these constant interruptions during worship, so he told Frank that if he just remained silent during the entire sermon, he would buy him a new pair of boots. Frank determined not to say a word in response to any good thing he heard from the pulpit, no matter how wonderful the preacher's declarations about God might be.

That Sunday it seemed that the preacher had some exceptionally good things to say about God and about what God had accomplished through Jesus. Poor Frank struggled hard to contain himself all during the service. Several times he almost forgot his promise to his master not to let go with a word of praise, but he kept his lips buttoned with the image of those new boots that would soon be his. Within his heart, however, there were shouts of Hallelujah!

At one point, the preacher said something so incredibly wonderful that Frank just couldn't remain silent. He stood up and shouted at the top of his lungs, "Boots or no boots—praise the Lord!"

Such is the unrestrained joy that fills us when the Spirit makes clear to us what God accomplished in Jesus Christ.

Tollbooth Joy

My son often said to me as he was growing up, "Dad, you're a nice guy, but you're dangerous." I knew what he meant. Sometimes I just can't restrain myself and I have to have fun, not only for my sake, but also for the people around about me.

There is a toll bridge that connects Palmyra, New Jersey with the Tacony section of Philadelphia. I crossed that bridge with great regularity back in the days when I was dating my wife-to-be. It only cost twenty-five cents to cross the bridge back then, and from time to time, when I could afford it, I would give the toll collector two quarters. Then I would tell the toll collector that I was paying for myself and also for my good friend in the car right behind me. I never really knew who was in the car behind me, but it was worth a quarter just to pull away from the toll booth, look in the rear-view mirror, and watch the toll taker trying to explain it to the next guy. If you don't understand what this has to do with the joy of the Lord, I don't suppose I can explain it to you.

Visible Joy

I seem to be particularly dangerous when I get on elevators. Our society teaches us to turn and face the doors and stand there quietly. But in my younger days, I loved to turn around and face the others in the elevator with me and say something like, "You're probably wondering why I called this meeting."

Once when I was in the elevator of a New York skyscraper filled with very serious-faced businesspeople, I smiled and said, "Lighten up. We're going to be traveling together for quite a while. What do you say we sing?" Incredibly, they did! I don't know whether they were intimidated by me or just wanted to have some fun, but businessmen with attaché cases in hand and businesswomen in their power suits joined me in singing, "You Are My Sunshine."

When I got off at the seventieth floor, one man got off and walked down the hall with me, wearing a big smile on his face. I asked him, "Are you going to the same meeting I'm going to?"

"Nah," he said. "I just wanted to finish the song."

In Archibald MacLeish's great play *J. B.,* Satan is asked what he misses most about heaven, and he answers, "The sound of the trumpets!"

Indeed, to be in the presence of God is to be part of a glorious celebration. Sometimes that is hard to grasp when I'm in the pulpit looking at the somber faces of those in the congregation. I hear them say, "We know the joy of the Lord." And I feel like saying, "Would you please notify your faces?"

Joyful Noise

For years I spoke at a Christian festival held in central Pennsylvania. This festival drew tens of thousands of young people and had a definite Pentecostal flavor to it.

The festival always reached a crescendo on the Saturday night, and on several of those occasions I was the featured speaker. One particular year I spoke on the Saturday night, and word got around the festival that I would be speaking at a nearby Lutheran church at the eleven o'clock hour on Sunday. Hundreds of charged-up young people from the festival came to the church that morning. The sanctuary was filled. Instead of the usual four to five hundred people, there were at least fifteen hundred squeezed into the auditorium and into the balcony.

This was a very "high" church. The minister was dressed in robes and there were all the smells and bells that accompany that kind of worship. As we walked onto the front platform of the church, the pastor noticed the huge crowd and whispered to me, "I'm not surprised. I put an ad in the newspaper." Little did he suspect what was about to happen.

The pastor took his place behind the pulpit and intoned in somber and solemn fashion, "This is the day that the Lord has made! Let us be glad in it! Let us enter into His gates with thanksgiving and into His courts with praise!"

At that point, some Pentecostal kid in the balcony yelled at the top of his lungs, "All right!" Young people all over the sanctuary started to clap and cheer.

It was more than humorous to watch the pastor's reaction. His knees actually buckled. He didn't know what to do! The last thing in the world he expected when he called upon the congregation to "make a joyful noise unto the Lord" was that anybody *would!*

The Spirit Leads Us

In Romans 8:14 we learn that the Holy Spirit leads us in our everyday lives, and that's good news. We constantly make decisions and we long for a prompting from God as to just what should be done. Sometimes these promptings aren't always as clear as we would like them to be. Sometimes we are so out of touch with God that we cannot discern them. However, there is no question but that the promise of God is that we will experience the leading of the Spirit at all times, if we will just be sensitive to it.

God Is My Copilot

If I were giving you directions to come to visit me, I could draw a map and describe for you the highways and roads that you should take to get to my house. I could tell you how far to go on each road and exactly where to turn. I could spell out the directions with details. But directions would not be as good as if someone were in the car with you who knew the way. Then, you wouldn't need a road map or directions because the person who knew the way could show you exactly where to go.

This is the work of the Holy Spirit. In John 14, Jesus told us that when He left us He would send to us the Holy Spirit, who would be the Comforter. In the Greek (out of which the New Testament is translated), this word "Comforter" can properly be translated as "copilot." It means "the one who comes alongside of us to assist us." That old line that says "God is my copilot" is not far from the truth.

Locomotive Lost

As a child, I remember hearing a story about a locomotive that did not want to stay on the tracks. It wanted to wander into the towns that it passed and into the beautiful fields it saw along the way.

One day the locomotive decided to leave the tracks, and he did! But when he wandered into town, he created great consternation among the people. The smoke that belched from the engine dirtied the clothes of the people of the town. The locomotive caused traffic jams and its enormous weight cracked the streets on which it rode.

When the locomotive went into the fields, to enjoy the flowers that he saw there, he immediately got bogged down. Farmers had to come with tractors and pull him out. Everywhere the locomotive went he caused trouble, and the more trouble he caused, the more miserable he became. Finally, the townspeople got him back on the track he was created to ride. It was then he discovered that he really could not be happy unless he was on track, following the route intended for him.

That cute little story is told to suggest that God has a track for each of us to follow in life. When we wander from that track, we cause chaos and sadness for others—as well as for ourselves. It is the work of the Holy Spirit to keep each of us on track and to keep us going in the direction that each should go.

Bicycle Built for Two

Almost every year, my wife makes sure that we go off to her favorite vacation spot in the whole world—Ocean City, New Jersey! One of the things I love to do is rent bicycles and ride on the boardwalk at this ocean resort. One day, I rented a bicycle built for two. I sat on the front seat and my wife sat on the backseat. After a short while, she told me that she didn't like this tandem bicycle because she couldn't steer it, and she really couldn't see where she was going. So we traded seats, and from then on she was in control, and *she* determined where we went. She liked it much better. I don't think we ever rented a tandem bike again.

In so many ways, I think our experience on that tandem bike is a parable about life. Each of us wants to be up front determining where we will go. What God wants is for each of us to take the backseat and allow Him to be in control. God promises that if we allow ourselves to be controlled by the Holy Spirit, we will be directed in the paths of righteousness and headed in the direction that is best.

Knowing the Author

In John 14:26, Jesus tells us that the Holy Spirit will come to us and lead us into all truth. Under the guidance of the Holy Spirit, we are able to grasp answers to some of the ultimate issues of our lives. Without the Holy Spirit, much remains ambiguous. This is certainly true of the Scriptures. The meaning of the Bible can be difficult to grasp, but it begins to speak to us in specific and direct ways when we allow the Holy Spirit to fill us and lead us as we read it.

When I was in high school, my mother gave me a book entitled *Silver Trumpet*, written by James Wesley Ingles. I read the book under my mother's orders, but it didn't really impress me very much. But a few years later, I enrolled at Eastern College in St. Davids, Pennsylvania, and to my surprise, my English teacher was James Wesley Ingles, himself. He proved to be one of the most inspiring teachers who ever taught me.

I went back and read *Silver Trumpet* a second time. During the second reading, I gained insights and inspiration I had not seen during the first reading. Of course, the difference was that I had gotten to know the author. When you know the author, everything about the book takes on new dimensions.

And so it is with the Bible. Until you know the author, God the Holy Spirit, you'll never get the inspiration and the truth that lies within its pages.

The Spirit Teaches Us How to Pray

Praying is too often reading off a list of nonnegotiable demands to the Almighty. We frequently treat God as though He was a genie who comes out of a magic lamp and grants us whatever we request, regardless of how selfish our requests may be. I remember so well my little boy coming into the living room just before going to bed and saying, "I'm going to bed! I'm going to be praying! . . . Anybody want anything?"

Or Else

Sometimes praying takes the form of bargaining. We tell God that if He delivers what we want, we will deliver what He wants in the way of good works. Sometimes it even takes on the character of blackmail.

The story is told of a little boy who, while saying his prayers, begged God for a new BMX bicycle. His mother corrected him and explained that prayer should not be an attempt to get our selfish desires met. Praying to God was no way to get a BMX bicycle.

It was the Christmas season, and when the boy's mother came down the steps the next morning, she noticed that something was missing from the manger scene under the Christmas tree. She was surprised to see that the little figurine of Mary was gone. In its place was a note that read, "Dear Jesus, If You ever want to see Your mother again, You had better get me that BMX bicycle!"

Someone's Not Listening

One of my favorite stories about prayer is about an elderly missionary who was discussing prayer at a women's conference. To the small circle of women gathered around her, she explained that when she first went to the mission field, more than fifty years earlier, she was extremely lonely. She saw that other missionaries were married and had families, and she bemoaned the feeling that she was all alone. In her loneliness, she begged God to pick out a husband for her. She told how she prayed and prayed and prayed, and was sure that God would answer her prayer.

One of the women in the group exclaimed, "But, you've never married! You're still single!"

The elderly missionary said, "You're right! But somewhere out there is a seventy-four-year-old man who has been resisting God's will for more than fifty years."

The story is not only funny, but it also drives home the point that we cannot expect God to manipulate people to our own personal ends.

Charlie Stoltzfus

When it comes to being led by the Spirit, sometimes there's a lot of fun to be had.

Several years ago I was invited to speak at a small Pentecostal college located near Eastern College, where I teach. I love going to this little school because the people there seem to be so in touch with the power of the Holy Spirit.

Before the chapel service, several of the faculty members took me into a side room to pray with me. I got down on my knees and the six of them put their hands on my head and prayed for me, asking the Holy Spirit to fill me up and use me effectively as I spoke to the students. Pentecostals seem to pray longer and with more dynamism than we Baptists do. These men prayed long, and the longer they prayed the more they leaned on my head. They prayed on and on and leaned harder and harder. One of them kept whispering, "Do you feel the Spirit? Do you feel the Spirit?" To tell the truth, I felt something right at the base of my neck, but I wasn't sure it was the Spirit.

One of the faculty members prayed at length about a particular man named Charlie Stoltzfus. That kind of ticked me off, and I thought to myself, *If you're going to lean on my head, the least you can do is pray for me.* He prayed on and on for this guy who was about to abandon his wife and three children. I can still hear him calling out, "Lord! Lord! Don't let that man leave his wife and children! Send an angel to bring that man back to his family. Don't let that family be destroyed! You know who I'm talking about, Lord . . . You know who I'm talking about . . . Charlie Stoltzfus. He lives down the road about a mile on the right-hand side in a silver house trailer!"

I thought to myself, with some degree of exasperation, *God knows where he lives . . . What do you think God's doing, sitting up there in heaven saying, "Give me that address again"?*

Following the chapel talk, I got in my car and headed home. I was getting on to the Pennsylvania turnpike when I saw a young man hitchhiking on the side of the road. I picked him up. (I know you're not supposed to, but I'm a Baptist preacher and whenever I can get someone locked in to where I can preach to him, I do it.) As we pulled back onto the highway I introduced myself. I said, "Hi, my name's Tony Campolo. What's your name?"

He said, "My name's Charlie Stoltzfus . . . "!

I didn't say a word. I drove down the turnpike, got off at the next exit, turned around, and headed back. When I did that, he looked at me and said, "Hey, mister! Where are you taking me?!"

I said, "I'm taking you HOME!"

He said, "Why?"

And I said, "Because you just left your wife and three children! RIGHT?"

He said, "RIGHT! RIGHT!"

He leaned against the passenger door the rest of the way, staring at me. I drove off the turnpike and onto a side road—straight to his silver house trailer. When I pulled into the drive, he looked at me with astonishment and said, "How did you know I lived here?"

I said, "God told me!"

Well, I believe that God did tell me. I think God may set up things like that, just for fun. I mean, if you're God, you're probably having a pretty sad time of it looking down on all the things that are going on in the world. I can just imagine God nudging Peter and saying, "Hey, Pete. Watch this!"

I told Charlie, "You get in that house trailer because I want to talk to you and I want to talk to your wife."

He ran into that mobile home ahead of me. I don't know what he said to his wife, but when I got in the house trailer her eyes were as wide as saucers. I sat them down and said, "I'm going to talk and you're going to listen."

Man, did they listen! And during the next hour I led both of them into a personal relationship with Jesus. Today that guy is a Pentecostal preacher down South.

When the Spirit leads, there are all kinds of surprises in store for us.

The Cost of Patience

A young Methodist pastor was visited by his bishop. Toward the end of the visit, the bishop asked, "Son, is there anything I can pray about on your behalf?"

"Yes," said the young pastor. "I don't have much patience with my congregation. I have visions and dreams and they don't seem to respond to them. They move too slowly, so far as I'm concerned, and I can't put up with them dragging their feet when I want to move the church forward. Please, Bishop, pray that God gives me patience."

The bishop and the young man walked to the front of the church, kneeled down at the altar and the bishop began to pray. "Dear Lord, bring tribulation into this young man's life! Bring suffering! Bring troubles! Create a host of trials for him."

The young pastor interrupted the bishop and said, "Stop! I wanted patience, not troubles and trials and tribulations."

The bishop then said, "But, son, the Bible tells us that tribulation worketh patience. If you want patience, you will discover that there's a price to be paid to get it. As life unfolds for you, its trials and tribulations will make you a patient man."

The Spirit Teaches Us to Forgive

When we pray the Lord's Prayer, we ask God to forgive us to the extent that we forgive other people. But forgiving others can be incredibly difficult. The good news is that the Holy Spirit comes into us as we surrender to God. And it is the Spirit that enables us to forgive like Christ forgives.

Forgive First

I once spoke at a church in South Jersey. As I stood up in the pulpit to preach, I noticed an elderly woman with a very mean expression sitting in the front row to my left. I immediately decided I would not preach to that side of the church.

If you've ever wondered why a preacher sometimes addresses his comments to one side of the church rather than the other, it may be there is some*one* from whom he turns away. That certainly was the case on this particular Sunday. However, when I decided to speak to the right side of the congregation, I realized there was another elderly woman in the front row on that side with an equally mean expression on her face, and she looked very much like the woman on my left. That Sunday I did most of my preaching to the center aisle!

After the service was over, I asked one of the deacons about those two mean-looking women. He told me they were sisters. I asked why one was sitting on one side of the church and the other was sitting on the other side of the church, and he told me they had had a little disagreement. When I responded by saying, "It's a good thing they don't live together," he answered, "They do!"

I didn't talk to either of these women, but if I had, I'm sure the one would have said, with her hand piously over her heart, "I'm a Christian woman! I'm willing to forgive my sister for what she did to me twenty-five years ago. But, Reverend, in the twenty-five years since that happened she has never once asked to be forgiven. Now, how can you forgive someone if that someone never asks to be forgiven?"

If I went to her sister, I'm sure I would get pretty much the same story. I can just hear her saying, "I'm willing to forgive my sister, but she's never asked to be forgiven!"

So they sit on opposite sides of the church, each waiting for the other to take the initiative to create reconciliation. The good news of the gospel is that Jesus did not wait for us to come to Him and ask for forgiveness. The Bible tells us that while we were yet in our sin He came and gave Himself on the cross. We have a God who, through the power of the Holy Spirit, can teach us to imitate Him and take the initiative by creating a spirit of forgiveness, restoring broken relationships.

Across the Divide

One of the most moving scenes I have ever witnessed occurred in Portadown, Northern Ireland. Two nights before the Orangemen were to march through the Catholic neighborhood taunting the people who lived there, a peace rally was held in the town hall, and I had been invited to participate.

The place was a beat-up old building, and the windows on one side were covered over with plywood because the glass had been shattered by bombs. Inside the hall, about a hundred people gathered, fairly evenly divided between Catholics and Protestants. During the hours that followed people from each side of the religious divide begged forgiveness from the other.

A Catholic man would tell of his wrong attitudes and confess to some mean and evil things that he had done to Protestants in years past. Then Protestants would call back to him saying, "We forgive you." A Protestant man would then confess to horrendous things he had done against Catholics. And this time the Catholics would respond by saying, "We forgive you." It went on and on like that until I was reduced to tears. The contrition, humility, and the prayers for forgiveness of that night were unparalleled in my experience.

Tomás Borge

An even more moving story of forgiveness is told about Tomás Borge, the Nicaraguan freedom fighter, who was a leader in the struggle against the totalitarian regime that had dominated his country.

During the revolution, Borge was captured and put in a dungeon. There he was chained to the wall, and in his helpless condition, was forced to watch as his captors dragged in his wife and gang raped her in front of him. Then they castrated him in an attempt to take away the last vestiges of his manhood.

When the revolution succeeded, Tomás Borge was released, and he paraded before the cheering crowds of Nicaragua as one of the nation's heroes. But as he marched, he noticed in the crowd the face of one of his captors. It was one of the men who had raped his wife.

Borge broke ranks from the parade, ran over to where the man was standing, grabbed him by the shoulders, shook him, and yelled, "Do you remember me? Do you remember me? Do you remember me?"

The trembling man pretended he had never seen Borge before. But Borge persisted and screamed, "I will never forget *your* face! I will never forget it!" Then he asked, "Now do you know what this revolution is all about? Now do you understand this revolution?"

The trembling and confused man could only answer in his fear, "Yes! Yes!"

Borge responded, "No! You don't understand what this revolution is all about!" Then he embraced the man and shouted, "I forgive you! I forgive you! That's what this revolution is all about!"

What an incredible story! It's a reflection of the forgiveness Christ gave us. We crucified Him. We put Him through hell because of our sins. Nevertheless, He embraces us and tells us about His revolutionary forgiveness, and extends to us His love.

Freedom

President Clinton tells of his first meeting with Nelson Mandela. In his conversation with this great leader of South Africa, the president said, "When you were released from prison, Mr. Mandela, I woke my daughter at three o'clock in the morning. I wanted her to see this historic event. As you marched from the cellblock across the yard to the gate of the prison, the camera focused in on your face. I have never seen such anger, and even hatred, in any man as was expressed on your face at that time. That's not the Nelson Mandela I know today. What was that all about?"

Mandela answered, "I'm surprised that you saw that, and I regret that the cameras caught my anger. As I walked across the courtyard that day I thought to myself, *They've taken everything from you that matters. Your cause is dead. Your family is gone. Your friends have been killed. Now they're releasing you, but there's nothing left for you out there.* And I hated them for what they had taken from me. Then, I sensed an inner voice saying to me, 'Nelson! For twenty-seven years you were their prisoner, but you were always a free man! Don't allow them to make you into a free man, only to turn you into their prisoner!'"

An unforgiving spirit creates bitterness in our souls and imprisons our spirits. A failure to forgive imprisons us.

True Love

There was a gruff and burly gunfighter with craggy facial features who lived in a frontier town. He never smiled, and he always seemed ready to kill anybody who crossed him. But one day the old gunfighter met a woman who took his fancy, and he began to date her. Standing in front of her house one evening, when he was saying goodnight, he blurted out, "Mary, I love you." The words just seemed to pop out. There was no attempt to make those words soft or dramatic. They were simply declared as a fact of life.

Mary stood there for a while, then slowly smiled and kissed the old gunfighter on the cheek, and said, "Joe! I love you too!"

Joe turned and walked slowly home. He went up the steps of the boarding house where he lived, closed the door of his room, got down on his knees at his bedside and prayed, "Dear God! I ain't got nothin' against nobody . . ."

Love does that to people—especially God's love.

To Forgive Each Other

Those who have been forgiven by the power of the Holy Spirit feel the forgiveness of God, and are by that same Spirit transformed into people who forgive others. All grudges disappear when the Spirit holds sway within our hearts. The forgiven become forgivers.

Chuck Colson, one-time White House counsel and founder of Prison Fellowship, tells the incredible story of taking a group of people into the Indiana State Penitentiary to conduct a worship service with inmates on death row. Following the service, as the visitors were checking out, it was discovered that one of them was missing. Colson hurried back to the cellblock to find that one of the men, part of the ministry team, was sitting in a cell with one of the prisoners with his arm around his shoulder. A bit ticked by this, Colson shouted at the man, "Don't you realize you're violating our privileges here? When we're asked to leave, we should leave! You can cause trouble for us by lingering behind like this."

The man looked up and said, "This brother is James Brewer. He's condemned to die. I'm Judge Clement. I'm the man who pronounced the sentence on him. Forgive me for lingering behind, but we both needed some time to forgive each other."

The Spirit Gives Us Dreams and Visions

Peter tells us that when the Holy Spirit fell upon the church on the day of Pentecost, it was the fulfillment of the Old Testament prophecies that old men and women shall dream dreams and the young shall have visions (Joel 2:28; Acts 2:17).

Things Hoped For

Faith is the substance of things hoped for and the evidence of things not seen. Our hopes and our dreams for the future help lift our humanity to the fullness of what it can be.

One of my favorite characters in the Bible is Abraham. He is in his late nineties when he has a vision. In my own imagination I can just see this old man waking up one morning, nudging his wife, and with a shaky voice saying, "Sarah? Sarah?"

The old lady, who was at least ninety-two, probably responded in groggy fashion, "What is it, Abe?"

"I just had a vision," says the old man.

"What kind of vision, Abe?" asks Sarah.

"I just had a vision of a new world! A new humanity! A new people! Sarah, you and I are going to create a whole new epoch in human history!"

"How does this new humanity start?" asks Sarah.

"Glad you asked!" smirks Abraham in response.

Imagine the next scene: It's this ninety-four-year-old man, probably limping along with a walker holding him up, alongside his ninety-two-year-old *pregnant* wife. (If you don't think God has a sense of humor, this should change your mind.)

"Where you going, Abe?" people ask.

"I don't know," the old man answers.

"Well then, why are you leaving?" they yelled back at him.

> ⌐ Helen Keller, the blind and deaf woman who made history by learning to overcome her disabilities, was once asked if there was anything worse than being blind. She answered, "Oh, yes! There is something worse than being blind. It is being able to see and not having any vision."

"BECAUSE GOD HAS GIVEN ME A VISION!" shouts Abraham.

Dreams and Visions

I was speaking at a special gathering of university students at UCLA. During the question-and-answer period, it was fairly obvious that these students had a sophomoric cynicism about them. They believed in nothing and no one. Toward the end of my exchange with them, I shouted out, "I'm sixty-two years old! Most of you are about twenty-two or twenty-three! And I am younger than you are. Because people are as young as their dreams and as old as their cynicism. I'm still dreaming, but you've given up on dreams and visions."

In Arthur Miller's remarkable play, *Death of a Salesman,* Willy Loman, the tragic character who dominates the play, is laid to rest in a cemetery following his suicide. At the graveside on a bleak and rainy day, the immediate family is huddled together along with a couple of friends. His wife cries softly over the casket, "Why? Why? Why did you do it, Willy?" It is then that Willy's son, Biff, speaks and says, "Aw, shucks, Mom. Aw, shucks. He had all the wrong dreams. He had all the wrong dreams."[2]

Again, it must be said that without dreams and visions, people perish.

Impossible Dreams

I was in a New York theater watching the musical *The Man of La Mancha*. Unexpectedly the woman next to me started whispering emphatically to her husband, "Stop that! Stop that! You're embarrassing me!"

I leaned forward and looked at her husband. He was a properly dressed man with all the symbols of upper-middle-class propriety, but he was sobbing uncontrollably. I knew why he was crying. It was because the man on the stage, Don Quixote, was singing the theme song "To Dream the Impossible Dream." He was singing about beating "the unbeatable foe" and striving with courage to go where the brave dare not go. He was singing to the audience that the world would be richer because "one man, bruised and covered with scars," still strove with all the courage he had to reach an unreachable star. The man was crying because he had lost his dreams. Somewhere along the line, he had lost his visions.

I don't know where you picked up your dreams and visions, but somewhere along the line God spoke to you. Perhaps it was at a Baptist revival meeting while singing for the twentieth time, "Just As I Am," or at a Presbyterian church retreat on the fiftieth verse of "Kumbayah"—but somewhere and someplace God spoke to you and gave you visions and dreams.

Interfering Facts

In that same musical, Don Quixote's somewhat ridiculous armor bearer and servant, Pancho Sanchez, stands with Don Quixote as they look at a tumble-down inn. Don Quixote waxes eloquent as to the beautiful castle that stands before them. He describes turrets and magnificent gates. In great detail, he describes the inn in terms that make it worthy of comparison to Alcazar. Pancho Sanchez squints his eyes and tries to see what Don Quixote sees, but in the end, he has to confess that all that lies before them is a tumble-down inn. He gives a careful description of what he sees, then Don Quixote silences him by yelling, "Stop! I will not allow your facts to interfere with my vision!"

When the Holy Spirit fills us, we have visions that defy the facts. Whenever I deal with young people who get a vision of doing something heroic for God, I can always count on their parents to throw cold water on it. Their parents often say they want them to be realistic. But such parents do not understand that when God takes possession of young people, He gives them dreams and visions that force them to look beyond the facts and sometimes run counter to reason. But we dare not turn them from these visions and dreams. They are what give meaning to our lives.

The Spirit Makes Us Fully Alive

Carpe Diem

A few years ago, I saw the film *The Dead Poets Society*, in which Robin Williams plays a teacher in an elitist private school. In one of the movie's initial scenes, he takes his students into the hallway of the school and has them stand before the trophy case. He points to a photograph of a football team from an early part of the century and tells the boys that if any of those players could speak to them now, they would say, "Carpe diem! Carpe diem!"

When he asks if anyone knows what *carpe diem* means, one of the boys tells him it is Latin for "seize the day." The rest of the story is about how these boys discover new dimensions in life by reading the poetry of the great English writers. They are sensitized and raised to a higher level of awareness than they had ever known before. They are led, by dead poets, to seize and live each day with passion.

As I watched the film, I was inspired by what was accomplished through poetry. But then I was convicted that even greater levels of passionate living could be achieved through the power of the Holy Spirit. In Romans 8:11 Paul tells us that the Holy Spirit makes us alive and lifts us out of the deadness of the past. This may be one of the most important dimensions of the new life in the Spirit and one that makes being filled with the Holy Spirit extremely attractive.

Are You Alive?

Several years ago, I taught a course at the University of Pennsylvania entitled, "Existentialism and Sociologism." One semester, on the first day of class, I pointed to an unsuspecting student and startled him when I asked, "How long have you lived?" The student was taken aback by the question and answered, "I'm twenty-two."

"No! No! No!" I said. "What you've told me is how long your heart has been pumping blood. My question was, how long have you lived?"

The student looked puzzled and couldn't quite grasp what I was talking about. I then told him this story of something special that happened to me when I was in the ninth grade and our school class took a trip to New York City.

We were taken to the top of the Empire State Building and, like most boys my age, I was chasing girls and crawling around the observation area. Then suddenly, I caught myself! I walked to the railing and peered over the edge of the building. The magnificence of the skyscrapers of New York lay before me and I stood there, stunned into reverence. In one mystical moment, I absorbed the city. I gazed at it with such intensity that if I were to live a million years that moment would still be part of my consciousness. I was so fully alive at that moment, that I sensed it had become part of my eternal now.

Then looking at the student, I again posed the question: "How long have you lived?"

My student answered pensively, "When you put it that way, Doc, maybe a couple of minutes. I don't know. It's hard to say. Most of my life has been the meaningless passage of time, between all too few moments of genuine aliveness."

No wonder the apostle Paul says in Romans the eighth chapter that we were once dead in the trespasses of sin but, through the power of the Holy Spirit, we have become fully alive. What Jesus wants for us is to be more alive to life, and to grasp all of its glorious potentialities. To help us to this end, we are given the Holy Spirit.

Really Alive

Fyodor Dostoevsky told the story of the time he was arrested by the czar, and sentenced to die. The czar played a cruel psychological trick on people who rebelled against his regime by blindfolding them and standing them in front of a firing squad. They heard gunshots go off but felt nothing, then slowly realized the guns were loaded with blanks.

The emotional trauma that went with the process of dying, without experiencing death, had a transforming effect on people. It certainly had an incredible effect on Dostoevsky. He talked about waking up the morning of his mock execution with full assurance that that would be the last day of his life. As he ate his last meal, he savored every bite. Every breath of air he took was taken with an awareness of how precious it was. Every face he saw that day he studied with intensity. He wanted every experience etched on his mind. As they marched him into the courtyard, he felt the sun beating down on him and he appreciated the warmth of the sun as never before. Everything around him seemed to have a magical quality to it. He was seeing the world as he had never been able to see it before. All of his senses were heightened. He was *fully* alive!

After his captors removed his blindfold and he realized he had not been shot, everything about him changed. He became grateful to people he had previously hated. He became thankful for everything about life, but especially for life itself. Dostoevsky claims that it was this experience that made him into a novelist and raised his sensitivities so that he could perceive dimensions of reality never known to him before.

The good news of the gospel is that we don't have to go through such trauma in order to be wakened to the joys of life. People apart from the Holy Spirit are often described in the Bible as being asleep, but it also tells us that the work of the Holy Spirit is to wake us up to all that life is about. In Romans 12:1, Paul tells us that we should approach life with our eyes wide open to the mercies of God. It is the Holy Spirit that opens our eyes to these mercies day in and day out.

Our Town

In Thornton Wilder's play *Our Town,* the main character, Emily, discovers the joy of being fully alive too late. After she is dead, she pleads with the spirits to allow her to return and look in on one day of her life, one last time. She picks her twelfth birthday.

Emily is more than dismayed as she recognizes how little the people she loves really comprehend the joys of life or experience them with any depth of awareness. She cries out to be taken away, to not have to watch any more of their inattention to the preciousness of life. Her parting words are, "Good-bye! Good-bye, world. Good-bye, Grover's Corners . . . Mama and Papa. Good-bye to clocks ticking . . . and Mama's sunflowers, and food and coffee. And even ironed dresses and hot baths . . . sleeping and waking up. O earth, you're too wonderful for anybody to realize you." She stoops, hesitates, and asks with tears in her eyes, "Do any human beings ever realize life while they live it? Eh? —, every minute?"[3]

That's a good question. The Holy Spirit is at work in us, trying to make us more alive every day. One mark of spiritual growth is an expanding awareness of the glories of our everyday experience—a growing sense of how precious the ordinary really is.

Bored

In the film *The Graduate*, Dustin Hoffman plays the role of a young man who has just finished his college career and is ready to move into the world of business. He is seduced by the infamous Mrs. Robinson, a friend of his family. As he is lying in bed with this older woman, he tries to engage her in a meaningful conversation. He tries to tell her about the great painters he learned about while at the university, but she's bored with it all. He then asks her what she majored in when she was in college. She answers, "Art."

It becomes obvious that this woman had lost her capacity for appreciating art and life itself. The intensity and awareness that had enabled her to enjoy great art was gone.

Sin deadens us to the ecstasies of life, but the Spirit of God gives us renewal.

> ↗ In the comic strip "Calvin and Hobbes," little Calvin on one occasion yells out, " I demand more than happiness! I demand EUPHORIA!"
>
> It may not be until we are with Christ in glory that the euphoric life will be fully realized. But that is the goal toward which we press. And it is to reach that goal that the Spirit comes to aid us.

5

What We Overhear
about Becoming a Christian

Becoming a Christian is a decision-making process. It involves a decision to believe what the Bible says is true. It requires a decision to commit yourself, without reservation, to what Christ wants you to be and do. And it is also a decision to surrender to being taken over by Jesus and yielding to the changes He wants to make in your life.

It's a Decision to Believe

Believe First

I was a guest speaker at an Ivy League university. The students that crowded into the lecture hall were intensely interested in the Bible and the gospel message. It was as though they wanted to believe and were hoping to hear some good reasons that would enable them to do so.

At the end of the lecture there was a question time, and the very first question was asked by a young man who stood and inquired, "How can you possibly believe that the Bible is true? You seem like an intelligent person, and you seem to be well-credentialed. How could anybody with your academic background possibly accept those Bible stories as though they were true?"

"Because I decided to!" I answered. "Many years ago, I considered the various options of truth that were available in the intellectual marketplace, and I made a decision to believe the Bible. Having made that decision, I spent the ensuing years constructing arguments and gathering information that would buttress my beliefs. But to be honest, I believed first. All my thinking and all my philosophizing and theologizing since then has been designed to support my *a priori* faith commitment."

The young man was taken aback by my forthrightness. He smiled and said, "I thought so."

"Before you sit down," I said to him, "I have a question to ask of you. Why *don't* you believe the Bible? Isn't it because you decided *not* to? Please, don't tell me you've read it from cover to cover, tested out what it has to say, and gained empirical evidence to contradict it. Please don't tell me that it's full of contradictions, because I don't think you can name five. I think that what you did was to decide a while back that the Bible was not true, and having made that decision, you've been constructing arguments and gathering information to support your *a priori* commitment to nonbelief. Let's be honest. I have as much basis for believing the Bible as you have for not believing."

Then I pulled out Blaise Pascal's argument called *The Great Wager*. I said to him, "If my faith commitment to what I believe to be true is erroneous, and there is no God and the Bible is false, I will not ever know it. When I die, all consciousness will cease to exist. On the other hand, if your atheism proves false, you *will* know it!"

Anthony Flew, the philosopher of logical positivism, once described two men walking through a forest. They came to a clearing where some flowers were growing up. The believer immediately pointed to them and said, "Look! There's been a gardener here. Look at all the flowers!"

The cynic said, "There has been no gardener. Look at all the weeds!"

The argument goes on and on. But it all boils down to the reality that the man who wanted to believe in the gardener had ample evidence to support his claims, as did the man who refused to believe there was a gardener. And so it is with arguments between believers and skeptics. Each can find evidence for *a priori* commitments.

Another Explanation

When I was in graduate school, I had the privilege of doing my doctoral dissertation under the prominent "God Is Dead" theologian Paul Van Buren. I owe a great deal to this man, because he was the first one who forced me to think in ways that could avoid ambiguities. On one occasion, Dr. Van Buren was trying to show me that my religious convictions would not stand up to any kind of empirical testing. He said, "If you want to convince the skeptics on this campus that your god is real, why don't you do what the Old Testament prophet Elijah did? Why don't you build an altar of wood and call down fire from heaven to consume it? Why don't you go out on Broad Street, stop the traffic, build up a high pile of logs, pour water all over it? Call all the doubters together, and when the crowd is properly assembled, call upon your god to rain down fire from heaven. Then you would have some empirical proof that God exists."

I answered by asking, "Dr. Van Buren, suppose I did that?

> The Bible has stood the test of time. Those who have tried to destroy it have failed. Archeology has borne out many of the things that are recorded there and the onslaught of modern science has not decimated its truth. There is no escape from its message. I love the story about W. C. Fields concerning the Bible. He was lying in a hospital bed very sick and near death, when his wife came in and found him reading the Bible. She exclaimed, "W. C.! What are you doing reading the Bible? I thought you didn't believe any of that stuff."
>
> W. C. Fields shot back, "Looking for loopholes, my dear. Looking for loopholes!"

Suppose I really did pile up some logs in the middle of Broad Street right in the midst of our university, and I called all the skeptics to come together and watch, just as Elijah once did with the skeptics of his age? Suppose, like Elijah, I poured water all over that pile of wood and called down fire from heaven—and fire did come down and consume the pile of wood. What would you say?"

My professor smiled wryly. "I would have to say—there *must* be another explanation!"

A Decision to Commit

Commitment

Believing is not enough. You have to make a commitment. J. Edwin Orr, a popular missiologist and evangelist, loved to speak to university students. When he had such an audience, he would usually pick out some young and innocent-looking woman, and ask her to stand. Then he would ask, "Do you believe in marriage?"

When the woman said, "Yes!" he would follow up by asking, "Why?"

The young woman would usually explain that she believed in marriage because it is an institution that gives stability to a sexual commitment, provides a good context for raising children, and provides an assurance of deliverance from loneliness throughout the life cycle. He would then declare, "You're married!"

The young woman could be counted on to protest and say, "No, I'm not!" to which Dr. Orr would point out that if she really *believed* in marriage, then it could be said that she *was* married.

The answer of the young woman was most often, "I haven't got a man yet, and I haven't made the commitment."

"Exactly!" Dr. Orr would respond. "It's not enough to believe! You have to make a commitment, and there has to be somebody to whom you make that commitment."

So it is with being a Christian. Affirming the truths of the Christian faith is not enough. A commitment must be made.

To Really Believe

Perhaps the most often-used story illustrating commitment is about Blondin, the famous French tightrope walker. In 1894, Blondin strung a tightrope across the Niagara Falls and, before thousands of cheering people, inched his way from the Canadian side to the United States side of the falls. When he arrived safely, the crowd cheered him. They yelled his name over and over again, "Blondin! Blondin! Blondin!"

Blondin shouted back at the crowd, "I am Blondin! Do you believe in me?"

The crowd responded by screaming, "We believe! We believe!"

Blondin then asked, "Do you believe that I can go back across the falls on that tightrope carrying someone on my shoulders?"

Again, the crowd yelled, "We believe! We believe!"

Blondin then asked, "Who will be that human being?"

There was dead silence. Then after an uncomfortable minute or two, a man stepped forward (it turned out to be Blondin's business manager). He climbed on Blondin's shoulders and allowed Blondin to precariously carry him back to the other side of the falls.

The point of the story is blatantly clear. Thousands yelled, "I believe! I believe!" But in the end, only one man *really* believed.

Go Out!

A story is told about a Coast Guard unit stationed at Cape May, New Jersey. One night a hurricane blew in from the Atlantic Ocean and a ship was breaking up just off the coast. The commander of the unit woke the men under his command and told them to prepare to go to sea. One of the young recruits shot back incredulously, "But, Captain! If we go out there, we may never come back."

The captain answered, "Son, you don't have to come back! You have to go out."

Being a Christian requires betting your life on the truth of the gospel and committing yourself with all the risks involved. It requires the abandonment of the securities that this world has to offer, and that you launch out into unknown waters where the threats are great.

Jump!

No one tells stories about commitment better than Sören Kierkegaard. That's probably because he saw commitment as being at the core of what it means to be a Christian.

Perhaps his most famous illustration of commitment is the tale he tells about a man trapped on the edge of a cliff with a raging fire burning toward him. It will only be a minute or two before the fire consumes him when he hears a voice from down below the cliff, amidst the darkness, calling, "Jump!"

The man answers, "But, I can't see you! There's only darkness down there!"

The voice from the deep shouts back, "Jump anyway. *I can see you!*"

Kierkegaard uses this story to illustrate what he called "the leap of faith." In the end, what is required in committing oneself to Christ is so overwhelming that only those who are desperate are ready to take that leap of faith and give themselves over completely to that voice that calls in the night.

Ducks

Perhaps my favorite Kierkegaardian story is his parable of the ducks. He describes a town where only ducks live. Every Sunday the ducks waddle out of their houses and waddle down Main Street to their church. They waddle into the sanctuary and squat in their proper pews. The duck choir waddles in and takes its place, then the duck minister comes forward and opens the duck Bible. (Ducks, like all other creatures on earth, seem to have their own special version of the Scriptures.) He reads to them: "Ducks! God has given you wings! With wings you can fly! With wings you can mount up and soar like eagles. No walls can confine you! No fences can hold you! You have wings. God has given you wings and you can fly like birds!"

All the ducks shouted, "Amen!" *And they all waddled home.*

How descriptive that story is of many church people. They hear of their potential in Christ. They agree with the declarations about the new life that can be theirs through a faith commitment. But in the end, they do not act upon what they have heard. They do not make the commitment. They simply say, "Amen!" and continue on in life as they always have.

Really Swimming

Kierkegaard also tells the story of a boy in a swimming pool trying to impress his father by pretending that he knows how to swim. He splashes and kicks the water with one foot and yells to his father, "Look! Look! I'm swimming!" He splashes with his arms and kicks with one leg, but he *isn't* swimming—because all the time he is holding on to the bottom of the pool with the big toe of his other foot.

How many of us call out to people around us, trying to impress them by saying we're Christians when we're not ready to let go of the world. We're not ready to totally commit ourselves. The boy wasn't swimming because he did not surrender to the water, and we are not Christians until we give ourselves over completely to Christ.

The Fire Chief

Most people who read Kierkegaard looking for stories are thrilled when they come across his tale about the fire chief. Kierkegaard told about a town that had a congenial man who led the fire brigade. Everyone thought of the fire chief as a gentleman of the highest order. Children loved to visit the firehouse and look over his equipment. He always tipped his hat to women when he passed them on the street, and he could be counted on for good conversation when men gathered on street corners.

But one day there was a fire! The fire chief rounded up his brigade, and they rushed to the building that had flames pouring from its windows. Much to his surprise, the fire chief couldn't get to the fire because interposed between him and the burning building were several hundred townspeople. Each of them was holding a water pistol, and from time to time, the people would smile at one another and squirt their pistols at the raging inferno. "What does the fire chief say?" asks Kierkegaard.

The fire chief yells, "What are you doing here? Why do you have water pistols? What are you trying to accomplish?"

The spokesman for the group answers, "We've all gathered here to support your efforts, sir! We all believe in the good work you do in this community, and each of us has come to make a humble contribution." With that the people in the crowd smile at each other, aim their water pistols at the fire, squeeze the triggers, and squirt some water at the flames.

"We all could be doing more," says the spokesman (Squirt! Squirt!). "Couldn't we, folks? (Squirt! Squirt!) But, the little that each of us can contribute we gladly give, just to show that we are with you" (Squirt! Squirt!).

"How does the fire chief respond?" asks Kierkegaard. The fire chief says, "Get out of here! Fires like this are not for well-meaning people who want to make limited contributions! Such situations demand firemen who are ready to risk their lives in putting out the flames!"

Kierkegaard makes it clear that going to church and making our small contributions to the work of the ministry from time to time might be nice, but so much more is required of us if we are to deal with life as true Christians.

A Decision to Do What Jesus Would Do

Becoming a Christian is a commitment to change. It is a decision to become the kind of person the Bible prescribes that Christians should be. No one can become a Christian without undergoing a radical transformation.

I'm Trying

A friend of mine tells the story of a derelict man, standing on a street corner in the Wall Street district of New York, begging for money. Reaching out his hand, he pleaded with a passing corporate executive with the words, "Change? Change?"

The corporate executive responded with a pained expression on his face, "I'm trying! I'm trying!"

Being a Christian isn't just changing once and for all. It is a commitment to change daily. The entire life of a Christian is one of pressing toward the mark of becoming the kind of person that Christ calls each of us to be (Phil. 3:13–14).

WWJD

More and more I see people wearing little pins that read WWJD. These letters refer to a phrase from Charles Sheldon's famous book *In His Steps*. Sheldon tells of a pastor who asks his congregation to commit themselves to doing whatever Jesus would do in any given situation. Before any of them say anything, each should ask, "If Jesus was in my place, what would He say? What would He do?" The Christian is then required to do what Jesus would do, with the help of the Holy Spirit. The rest of the book is simply an account of the amazing things that happen in this little town as people follow this simple directive for living the Christian life.

I remember reading that book when I was senior in high school. It challenged me greatly. I went to school the next day determined to do what Jesus would do if Jesus was in my place.

I was a ballplayer. In every sense I was what kids today would call a jock. Like most high-school jocks, I was on somewhat of an ego trip. At school I loved to walk down the hall to my homeroom. It was

Homeroom 48! That means nothing to you, but to those in West Philadelphia it had great significance, because Homeroom 48 was the one to which the jocks were assigned. I imagined myself walking down that hall with girls lining the walls singing, "How Great Thou Art!"

When I got to my homeroom, I looked over my array of friends and then realized there were five guys in the room that I wished weren't there. They were members of the chess team. Now, I have nothing against chess players, mind you. As a matter of fact, some of my best friends are chess players! It's just that these guys were wimps. If that doesn't translate, perhaps the word "nerds" will do. I usually tried to stay away from them and sit with the big-shot jocks in the room, but then I asked myself, "What would Jesus do?" I knew the answer. I went and sat next to one of the nerds.

It turned out to be the smartest move I made during my high-school years. The guy was brilliant in algebra. He carried me my whole senior year. But more than that, he turned out to be the most interesting and witty guy I met in high school. Later on, I realized just how much I had allowed socially created stereotypes to determine my friendships. I realized how much prejudicial impressions had kept me from getting to know some people who were extra special.

I wish this story had one of those wonderful endings that evangelists give to stories like this. Then I would declare: "Because I loved that wimp, because I cared for that wimp, today that wimp is one of the great leaders of our nation!"

But that's not the case. He's just an ordinary man with an extra-ordinary wit. And if anybody calls my friend a wimp today, he'll have to deal with me.

A Party Dress

A friend of mine, who is an associate pastor of a large Presbyterian church in California, once told me how she loved to go to Nordstrom department store in Bel Air during the Christmas season. She couldn't afford to buy much at that store, but she enjoyed going there at

Christmas time just to take in the ambiance. The Christmas decorations were always magnificent, and there was live music on several floors.

On one of her visits, my friend was on the top floor of the store looking at some of the finest dresses in the world, when the elevator doors opened and out stepped a bag lady. Her clothes were dirty and her stockings were rolled down to her ankles. She just stood there holding a gym bag in her right hand. It was obvious that this woman was out of place and not about to buy anything. The dresses were in the thousand-dollar category, and this bag lady did not seem like the kind of person who would have that kind of money.

My friend expected a security guard to promptly arrive and usher the bag lady out of the store. But instead of security guards, a stately saleswoman came over to her and asked, "May I help you, madam?"

The bag lady said, "Yeah! I wanna buy a dress."

"What kind of dress?" the saleswoman asked in a polite and dignified manner.

"A party dress!" the bag lady answered.

"You've come to the right place," said the saleswoman. "Follow me. I think we have some of the finest party dresses in the world."

The saleswoman then spent more than ten minutes matching dresses with the woman's skin color and eye color, trying to help her ascertain which dress would go best with her complexion. After selecting three dresses that the saleswoman deemed to be most appropriate for the bag lady, she bade the woman to follow her into the dressing room. My friend hurried into the adjoining dressing room and put her ear up to the wall. She wanted to hear all of this. It was remarkable!

The bag lady tried on the dresses with the saleswoman's help. But then, after about ten minutes, the bag lady said sternly, "I've changed my mind. I'm not going to buy a dress today!"

"That's okay," the saleswoman said gently. "But here's my card. Should you come back to Nordstrom department store, I do hope that you will ask for me. I would consider it such a privilege to wait on you again."

This, of course, is a brilliant illustration of what Jesus would do, if Jesus was a saleswoman in Nordstrom.

The Wrong Answer

A friend of mine told me about being at dinner with a veteran of World War II. As they talked, the man related a story of what it was like during the famous Battle of the Bulge. He described how one foggy, rainy morning his commanding officer commanded his unit to go out and shoot any of the enemy that were lying about wounded. Of course, this did not fit in with the Geneva Convention, but given the confusion and disarray of a battle in which there were no clearly drawn lines, the officer believed that it had to be done. In this battle the rules had been abandoned, and prisoners were not to be taken.

The veteran then told about coming upon a German soldier sitting on the ground with his back against a tree. He wasn't wounded. He was just too tired to go on. He was totally dissipated. There was nothing left in the way of will power. He was too listless and tired to resist anything or anyone. The man telling the story said, "As I aimed my gun at him, he asked me to wait a moment. Speaking in English, he told me he wanted a chance to pray before he died. I immediately sat down with him as I realized that he was a Christian brother. We talked about our families. I showed him pictures of my children. He showed me photographs of his family. We read some Scripture together. It was wonderful."

My friend asked, "Well? What did you do?" When the man didn't answer, my friend kept pressing. "What did you do? What did you do?"

The man said, "I stood up, aimed the gun at him, and said, 'You're a Christian and I'm a Christian. I'll see you in heaven.' And I shot him!"

This man might say that he was acting under orders. It might justify his actions in a multiplicity of ways, but in the end he can never tell himself that what he did is what Jesus would have done, if Jesus had been in his place. Being a Christian is more than just believing in Christ. It is giving the right answer to the question What would Jesus do?

When You Grow Up

A study done on mothers around the world asked the question, "What do you want your children to be when they grow up?" Mothers in Japan almost always answered, "We want our children to be *success-ful.*" The result is that the people of Japan have raised up a generation of the most success-driven children in the history of the world. They work harder and longer than any other people at any task assigned to them. They can be expected to excel in any activity they undertake. The way in which Japan recovered after World War II was largely due to the success orientation that was drilled into the children by their parents.

When American mothers were asked exactly the same question, you can imagine what the answer was: "We want our children to be *happy!*"

HAPPY?!?!?!

You've got to understand, I was raised in an old-fashioned Italian family. I don't think my father really *cared* whether I was happy. Oh, I suppose it was of concern to him, and I'm sure that he also wanted me to be successful. But if you had asked my father, and especially my mother, "What do you want your son to be when he grows up?" both would have answered, "We want him to be *good!*"

'Til Death Do Us Part

I have a friend who, at the pinnacle of his career, resigned a key leadership role at a Christian university in order to take care of his wife who suffered from Alzheimer's disease. The woman was in her early fifties, and if you know anything about that disease, you know that if it attacks people in their fifties, disintegration of the mind occurs rapidly. It wasn't long before her mind was gone. Not only was she incapable of recognizing her husband, she could not even recognize herself when she looked into a mirror. Her husband had to feed her. She lost the capacity to speak. She drooled and made slobbering sounds. Nevertheless, he cared for her, day in and day out.

His friends tried to convince him to put her into an institution where she could get proper care. They urged him to put her in a place where her basic needs would be met, and where people would kindly attend to her requirements for comfort. They pleaded with him not to give up his career and waste his time caring for her. They begged him not to turn away from what was an important ministry to the church, and kept reminding him, "She doesn't know who you are! She really doesn't recognize you! She doesn't know who you are!" Then someone laid the ultimate guilt trip on him by saying, "You're reneging on your calling from God!"

His answer was remarkable. He said, "You're right! She doesn't know who I am. But, I know who she is! And furthermore, there's only one thing that takes precedence over a calling from God—and that's a promise. And I promised her that I would be there until death do us part.

I don't think he's a *happy* man, but I am convinced that he's a *good* man. Being good is more important than being happy, and there are times we must be ready to forfeit our happiness in order to do the good that is required of us. Certainly, that is what Jesus would do.

He Had to Die

The story is told of a young lieutenant in World War II whose unit was ambushed by Nazi soldiers. Almost all of them escaped from the flying bullets by running into an old farmhouse. However, out of the darkness came the moans and groans of one of the men who had been severely wounded. The young lieutenant did the heroic thing. He crawled out into the night, grabbed the young recruit, and dragged him to the safety of the farmhouse. He saved the man, but even as he himself was going through the door to safety, he was struck by a bullet to his head and killed instantly.

A year or so later the young man for whom the lieutenant had heroically given his life was back in the States. The parents of the dead hero asked to meet him. On the appointed night, the soldier came to meet the mother and father of the man who had died for him. But when he arrived at the house where they lived, it was obvious to the parents of the dead hero that he was drunk.

They sat at dinner and tried to make conversation, but the man was loud and at times, obscene. Toward the end of the meal he vomited! The parents did the best they could do to make their way through a horrendous evening of suffering.

When the young soldier left, and they closed the door behind him, the mother of the dead hero slumped against the wall and moaned, "To think that our precious son had to die for somebody like that."

I'm sure that when the angels in heaven look upon the behavior of the likes of someone like me, they must say to one another, "To think that our precious Son had to die for somebody like that." I owe Him better! He gave His life for me and I should be ready and willing to do what He would do if He was in my place.

Learn by Seeing

One of the most impressive men of our time is Dr. Paul Brandt, the Baptist missionary to India. He was a surgeon, and during his years of ministry he performed eye operations that saved the vision of thousands of people. One day, he was taking a visitor on a tour of the hospital when he noticed one of his young interns talking intently to a patient. Dr. Brandt stopped and, in sheer amazement, said to the visitor, "Look at his face! Look at the expression on his face! There is only one other man I've ever known who could look at a person with such loving intensity. That was my teacher at medical school, the doctor under whom I interned. I haven't seen an expression like that since I was with him."

The visitor smiled and said, "But, Dr. Brandt, I have seen you care for patients, and whether or not you realize it, you have that exact expression on your face when a patient is telling you about suffering and pain."

That's the way it is when we imitate Christ and do what He would do. We become more and more like Him, and we set patterns that are imitated by those who come after us.

Every Day?

The story is told by M. Scott Peck, the famous psychologist and author, of a woman patient who was suffering from extreme depression. One day, when she was due for an appointment with him, she called on the telephone and told him that her car had broken down. Dr. Peck offered to pick her up on his way into work, but he explained to her that he had to make a hospital call before he got to the office. If she was willing to wait in the car while he made the call, they could have their appointment. She agreed.

When they got to the hospital, he had another suggestion. He gave her the names of two of his patients who were convalescing there, and told her that each of them would enjoy a visit from her. When they met again, an hour and a half later, the woman was on an emotional high. She told Dr. Peck that making the visits and trying to cheer up those patients had lifted her spirits, and that she was feeling absolutely wonderful.

Dr. Peck responded by saying, "Well, now we know how to get you out of your depression. Now we know the cure for your problem."

The woman answered, "You don't expect me to do that every day, do you?"

That's the tragedy of our lives. Doing what Jesus would do lifts us out of our doldrums into a higher quality of life. And yet, we often think that imitating Jesus is something burdensome. It's not! Doing what Jesus would do feeds us emotionally and lifts our spirits. One experiences the flow of the Spirit in the context of ministry.

What He Did for Me

A preacher was leaving Victoria Station in London. Sitting across from him in the little train compartment were two men in their late thirties. About ten minutes out of the station, one of the men had an epileptic seizure. His eyes rolled back and his body trembled. The man rolled off the seat onto the floor and shook uncontrollably. It was a shocking thing to see. His friend lifted the stricken man up and put him back onto the seat, took off his overcoat, and put it around him as a blanket. He rolled up a newspaper and put it in his mouth, lest the man bite his tongue. Then with great compassion, he lovingly blotted the beads of perspiration on the epileptic man's forehead. After a few minutes, the seizure ended with the same abruptness with which it began, and the stricken man dropped into a deep sleep. It was then that his friend turned to the preacher and said, "You'll have to forgive us. He doesn't have these seizures very often, but we never know when they're going to strike him.

"We were in Vietnam together," he continued. "We were both wounded. I lost a leg." Pointing to his right leg he said, "This is an artificial leg. I've learned to walk on it very well. My friend here had half of his chest blown away by a hand grenade. There was shrapnel all through his chest, and every time he moved he experienced great pain.

"The helicopter that was supposed to rescue us was blown out of the sky by an enemy rocket, and with that explosion we knew that all hope for rescue was gone. It was then that my friend somehow picked himself up. He screamed in pain with every move he made, but somehow he stood to his feet. Then he reached down and grabbed hold of my shirt and started pulling me through the jungle. I tried to tell him to give up on me. I pleaded with him to save himself if he could, and I kept telling him there was no way he was going to get us both out of the jungle. I'll never forget him saying, 'Jack, if you die in this jungle, I'm going to die here with you.' I don't know how he did it, mister, but step by step, scream by scream, he pulled me out of that mess. He saved my life!

"A year ago I found out that he had this condition and that somebody had to be with him all the time. So I closed down my condo in New York, sold my car, and came over here to take care of him. That's our story. I hope you understand."

My friend responded by saying, "Don't apologize. I'm a preacher.

Whenever I come upon a good story, I'm thrilled. And, this is one of the best stories I've heard in a long, long time."

His new friend on the other side of the compartment said, "Hey! Don't be impressed. You see, after what he did for me, there isn't anything I wouldn't do for him."

The Christian is someone who recognizes what Jesus did on the cross to accomplish salvation, and in response says to Jesus, "After what You did for me, there isn't anything I wouldn't do for You." That, of course, involves doing what Jesus would do if Jesus was in your place.

For Love

The story is told of Richard Bellinger, a young boy in South Carolina who was the son of a Baptist minister. One Saturday night Richard decided to shine his father's shoes. The following night his father put a silver dollar on the bureau of his son's room with a note commending his son for what he had done, and telling him that the dollar was his reward.

The next morning, when the father put on his shoes, he felt something hard and metallic in one of them. When he took the shoe off and reached inside, he found the silver dollar he had given to his son the night before. Along with the dollar was a note that simply read, "I did it for love!"

To be a Christian is to love Jesus so much that you want to be like Him. To be a Christian is to try to do what Jesus would do, not for reward, but out of loving gratitude for all that Christ has done for you.

A Decision to Surrender

Becoming a Christian involves more than *doing* something for Christ. What it really involves is realizing that His love for you is such that you don't have to *do* anything at all to earn His salvation. He gives it to you as a gift. As the Bible says so forthrightly, "By grace are ye saved through faith; . . . not of works, lest any man should boast" (Eph. 2:8–9). The Jesus I have been talking about is a living presence with you at this very moment. What He wants is for you to quietly surrender to Him. Be still and know that He is God! For as it says in Isaiah 30:15, "In returning and rest shall ye be saved; in quietness and in confidence shall be your strength."

In the Garden

When I was a teenager, I hated Sunday evening services. Sunday morning wasn't so bad. The sermon had some form and structure to it. I could generally count on three points and a poem. But in the evening, the preacher wasn't prepared. I knew that because he was all over the place giving every evidence that his sermon was "shooting from the hip." If that wasn't bad enough, it was fairly obvious he hadn't even taken the time to pick out the hymns for the evening service, because he always asked, "Does anybody have a favorite?"

Mrs. Kirkpatrick, who sat about five rows back from the front on the right-hand side of the church, could always be counted on to call out, "One-thirty in the green hymnal!"

> ↝ Someone once asked Mother Teresa, "When you pray, what do you say to God?"
>
> Her answer startled the interviewer. She said, "I don't say anything. I listen!" Not knowing how to answer, he fumbled around for words and finally said, "Okay! When you pray, what does God say to you?"
>
> Mother Teresa answered, "He doesn't say anything. He listens. And if you don't understand that, I can't explain it to you."

As a kid who pretended to be macho, I hated that hymn. You have to realize that I grew up on the streets of West Philadelphia, where survival depended on looking tough and acting tough, so as to scare away predators. I tried to walk in a cool manner and carry myself as though I were a rough-and-tumble guy. Given those realities, you can understand why I did not like one-thirty in the green hymnal. The hymn was "In the Garden." The words just didn't go with my attempted macho persona.

I can still hear the congregation singing, "I come to the garden alone, while the dew is still on the roses . . ."

The song just sounded far too effeminate for me. The second verse seemed even worse, "He speaks, and the sound of His voice is so sweet the birds hush their singing . . ."

I just couldn't sing that old gospel song. It just wasn't in me.

But that's because I was a kid. I've got to tell you that the older I get, the more I have grown to love one-thirty in the old green hymn book. The older I get, the more my attitude changes, and the more I love to sing that song. I especially love the chorus that goes:

> And He walks with me, and He talks with me,
> And He tells me I am His own.
> And the joy we share, as we tarry there,
> None other has ever known.[4]

Being a Christian for me is going to the quiet place and shutting out the world, and waiting patiently for Christ to reach out and love me. And then I love Him back.

The old Celtic Christians used to talk about going to a "thin place." By that they meant a place where the wall separating you from God is so thin that the love of God is able to flow through and envelop you. When was the last time you gave God even ten minutes of silence? When was the last time you gave Him fifteen minutes of stillness? When was the last time you said nothing at all to God, but in quietude yielded to His love? If God doesn't seem real to you, it may be because you haven't provided Him with a quiet time in which He can embrace you with His love and fill you with His presence. If you give Him silence, you will find that on the other side of silence, there is God.

6

What We Overhear about How to Live the Christian Life

There is little doubt that being a Christian requires some specific disciplines on our part, and that's what this chapter is all about. It contains some of the directives of Jesus that we are expected to follow. Any true Christian reading the Scriptures will overhear these directives and immediately begin to apply them to his or her heart.

Join a Support Group

We Leak

The story is told of an old guy in the backwoods of Kentucky who could be counted on to show up at revival meetings whenever an evangelist came to town. At the end of each service when the invitation was given, he would come down the aisle, get down on his knees, raise his arms to heaven and cry out, "Fill me, Jesus! Fill me! Fill me, Jesus!" Then, within a matter of a week or two, he would slip back into his old ways of living. But when the next round of revival meetings was held, he would once again go to the meetings, walk down the aisle, and pray the same prayer over and over.

One time, he was down on his knees yelling to the ceiling, "Fill me! Fill me, Jesus! Fill me, fill me! Fill me, Jesus!" when suddenly from the back of the church some lady yelled, "Don't do it, Lord! He leaks!"

Of course, the truth is that we all leak. Being filled spiritually is not a once-and-for-all thing. Our spiritual energies dissipate, and we must find ways to be regularly refilled by the Spirit and reenergized by God.

Filling Up

One of the primary means to experience regular renewal is by being a part of a small group. There are those who call them "support groups." Others call them "accountability groups." But I believe that everyone should belong to a group with two or three other people who meet regularly. I, myself, have such a group that meets for prayer and fun on Tuesday mornings. We meet at Joe's, an old-fashioned breakfast place that's close to where we live. When we get together, we talk about what's going on in our lives and listen to one another's troubles. In the context of intimacy, there is something of God's Spirit that flows between us and energizes each of us.

The New Testament gives evidence that Jesus had such a support group. You can name His partners. They were Peter, James, and John.

Church historians tell us that John Wesley had such a group at Oxford University. He and his friends met so methodically that the other students at Oxford ridiculed them and called them "The Methodists." That's where the name of that denomination came from. Testimonies about spiritual renewal are countless, but among those who have "made it" as Christians, most consider the dynamism of the Spirit experienced in small-group encounters to be a primary instrument for the maintenance of their faith.

Whatever spirituality we have eventually leaks out of us, but God wants to pour in His Spirit faster than it can ebb away.

The Whole Armor

It is through small groups that Christians take on the whole armor of God as described in Ephesians 6. Through such accountability groups we are encouraged to:

Take unto you the whole armour of God, that ye may be able to withstand in the evil day, and having done all, to stand. Stand therefore, having your loins girt about with truth, and having on the breastplate of righteousness: And your feet shod with the preparation of the gospel of peace; Above all, taking the shield of faith, wherewith ye shall be able to quench all the fiery darts of the wicked. And take the helmet of salvation, and the sword of the Spirit, which is the word of God. (Eph. 6:13–17)

I say all of this because I remember an African-American preacher I once heard on the radio telling his congregation that he didn't want any Christian streakers running around his church. I was intrigued by that statement. But he went on to explain that Christian streakers are those who are wearing only "the helmet of salvation." He wanted the people in his congregation to have the whole armor of God.

Adopt a Radical Lifestyle

Preachers seldom want to talk about the cost of discipleship. At one point in His preaching career, Jesus had more than five thousand followers, but when He preached one particular sermon, He alienated all but twelve of them. It was the sermon in which He spelled out the cost of discipleship. After His followers heard what was expected of them, and what it would cost them, most of them left Him. Only the twelve apostles remained, and He turned to them and asked, "How come you guys are still hanging around here?" It was then that Peter answered, "We don't have any place to go!" We are saved by grace, but if we want to become true disciples, the expectations are high.

So?

One time I was in Haiti with my son, Bart, who was then just seventeen years old. We were walking down one of the main streets of Port-au-Prince when we found ourselves surrounded by impoverished, raggedy children. They were begging for pennies, and I said, "Bart, don't give them anything! If you do, they won't let up until they've got every dime we have."

My son looked at me quizzically and answered, "So?"

What a fascinating and convicting answer! My son was letting it be known that being a Christian was to render all of life's resources to meet the needs of others in the name of Christ.

This Is Easy

In the movie *Beckett*, Richard Burton plays the role of that heroic archbishop of Canterbury. When this one-time libertine is ordained archbishop he goes through a ceremony in which he must divest himself of all his earthly goods. He invites the poor to come into the cathedral and then distributes his material possessions, item by item, among them. At one point he stops, points to the image of Jesus on the crucifix that hangs over the altar, and whispers harshly with an irony in his voice, "You! You! You are the only One who knows how easy this is! Everyone else thinks it is difficult!"

In that brilliant scene one gets the message that spirituality leads to sacrifice, but the sacrifices are easy because of the joy and fulfillment that comes from giving away one's earthly possessions to meet the needs of the poor. I am still struggling to learn the fullness of that joy. Somehow I still think, in spite of all Jesus has told me, that there is more joy in keeping things than in giving them away. I've got a lot to learn.

Jesus Was a Nigger

In one of the most dramatic sermons ever given at Eastern College, a prominent African-American theologian shocked the audience with his description of Jesus. He started off his message by saying, "Jesus was a nigger!" Then he went on to explain that he was not suggesting that Jesus had black skin. Being a nigger, he said, had to do with what you were in the eyes of the world. As a matter of fact, he pointed out, there are some African-American people who call other black people niggers. The word "nigger," he claimed, refers to the downtrodden, the spat upon, the cursed, the humiliated, the rejected, and the despised. Given that definition, he reasserted his contention that Jesus was a nigger. He went on to say, "There's no way you can read the fifty-third chapter of Isaiah and not come to this conclusion. There the prophet tells us that the Messiah would be despised and rejected; spat upon and cursed—and we would hide our faces from Him."

He then went on to make another statement that was almost as shocking as the first. He said, "If you want to be like Christ, then you must be ready to become a nigger too! You must be ready to empty yourself of the wealth, status, and power that has marked your life. But if you are thinking of turning away from this calling, you should be aware that only niggers can be saved!"

Who We Are

In the movie *Civil Action,* John Travolta plays the role of a lawyer representing the plaintiffs in a civil suit brought against a large corporation because of that company's irresponsible polluting of the environment. Chemical waste is being dumped into the rivers in a particular town in Massachusetts, causing cancer to break out among the townspeople.

Unfortunately, this lawyer and his small firm are no match for the tremendous legal services the corporation can buy. Little by little, the corporation exhausts the lawyer's financial resources and destroys his firm. In one highly dramatic scene, the lawyer stands before a bankruptcy judge and declares that fourteen dollars and a portable radio are all the possessions he has left in the world. The judge responds in amazement, "Where are all the things that you should accumulate in life in order to give you your identity?"

That simple line speaks volumes. That is exactly how the world in which we live evaluates the worth of an individual. Money and things establish a person's identity.

For Christians, things and the things money can buy do not establish identity. Instead, Christ does that. By giving ourselves away, and sacrificing all we have for Christ and the Kingdom, we establish who we are and find the significance of our lives.

Who We Should Be

While teaching at the University of Pennsylvania, I became good friends with a young Jewish student who eventually made a commitment to Christ. As I tried to mentor him and give him direction as to how to live the Christian life, I advised him to go to a particular church that was well known for its biblically based preaching, to help him get a better handle on what the Bible is all about.

When I met my friend several weeks later, he said to me, "You know, if you put together a committee and asked them to take the Beatitudes and create a religion that contradicted every one of them, you would come pretty close to what I'm hearing down there at that church. Whereas Jesus said, 'Blessed are the poor,' down there they make it clear that it is the rich who are blessed.

"Jesus said, 'Blessed are they that mourn,' but the people at that church have a religion that promises happiness with no crucifixions.

"Whereas Jesus talked about the meek being blessed, they talk as if they took assertiveness-training courses. Jesus may have talked about the merciful and peacemakers, but those people are the most enthusiastic supporters of American militarism and capital punishment I have ever met.

"Jesus may have lifted up those who endured persecution because they dared to embrace a radical gospel, but that church declares a gospel that espouses middle-class success and affirms a lifestyle marked by social prestige."

As I listened to my friend's accusing words about the church, I realized that it could just as well be aimed at me. Since that conversation, I've spent a lot of time reflecting on whether or not my lifestyle is really Christian.

Sören Kierkegaard once said, "If you mean by Christian what the Sermon on the Mount says about being a Christian, then in any given time in history, there might be four or five such persons who would have the right to call themselves Christians."

Passerby

I was standing on a street corner waiting for a bus in front of a church in downtown Philadelphia. People in cars were honking their horns impatiently in the busy traffic. On the sidewalks there were hustling, bustling pedestrians on their way home from work; others were going shopping. In the midst of all of this hectic activity, I happened to turn toward the church, which had a crucifix positioned about six feet above street level. Beneath the statue of the crucified Jesus were the simple words from Scripture, "Does it mean nothing to you, oh ye who pass by?"

Caught up in the round of activities that mark our lives, we are so much a part of the ways of this world, we forget that Jesus sacrificed everything for us and that we ought to be ready to sacrifice everything we are and have for Him. When I think about that, I realize that I've got a long way to go before I can truly call myself a follower of Jesus Christ.

Called to Witness and to Evangelize

Witnessing is something we are obligated to do. Christ commands us to evangelize the world, and anyone who has been filled with the Holy Spirit cannot help but be committed to the task of evangelism and sharing the gospel with the rest of the world.

What You Believe

On July 4, 1854, Charlie Peace, a well-known criminal in London, was hung. The Anglican church, which had a ceremony for everything, even had a ceremony for hanging people. So when Charlie Peace was marched to the gallows, a priest marched behind him and read these words from the Prayer Book:

"Those who die without Christ experience hell, which is the pain of forever dying without the release which death itself can bring."

When these chilling words were read, Charlie Peace stopped in his tracks, turned to the priest, and shouted in his face, "Do you believe that? Do you believe that?"

The priest, taken aback by this sudden verbal assault, stammered for a moment and then said, "Well . . . I . . . suppose I do."

"Well, I don't," said Charlie. "But if I did, I'd get down on my hands and knees and crawl all over Great Britain, even if it were paved with pieces of broken glass, if I could just rescue one person from what you just told me."

It is so easy for those of us in the evangelical community to talk about people going to hell. But if in the depths of our being we really believe this, we should

> ⌁ If you had the cure to cancer and kept that cure a secret for yourself, you would be among all people most despicable. If you had the formula for a medicine that would deliver people from that dreaded disease and did not share it, you would be deserving of the worst condemnation imaginable.
>
> But what about the fact that you know the cure for sin and spiritual death, and do not tell others about it? Are you not guilty of an even more hideous crime?

constantly be witnessing, because the thought of people going to hell without having heard about Christ should be an intolerable burden to bear.

No Training Necessary

There are those who will say that in order to share the gospel story an individual needs special training. To do it right, many would argue, requires the skills necessary to properly talk about the damnation people will experience apart from Jesus.

As you think about that, imagine yourself on a ship that is sinking because of a huge gash ripped on the underside of the hull. You look on this catastrophic situation, shrug your shoulders and say, "I suppose I ought to tell people that the ship is sinking, but I've had no special training in this sort of thing. I believe they were once offering a course on how to tell people what to do when a ship is sinking, but I didn't have a chance to take it. I have no experience in this sort of thing, so I think I'd just better leave the whole matter in the hands of others."

That would be absurd. One doesn't need special training for such a task. The fact that you know of the disaster and the impending death that goes with it is enough. Simply run to the upper decks and yell, "Save yourselves! Save yourselves!" Nothing more would be required.

If You Died Tonight

A minister tells the story of a man who stood up in a midweek prayer service at his church and gave a testimony. "I was at King's Cross in Sydney, Australia," the man said, "waiting for the traffic light to change. As I stood there, someone tugged on my jacket, and when I turned, this shabby-looking man looked at me and asked, 'Sir! If you were to die tonight, where would you spend eternity?' That question haunted me for more than three weeks. I could get no rest as it came back to me time and time again. I had to find an answer to it, and I found that answer in Jesus."

A couple of years later, another man stood in that same church and gave a testimony that had an incredibly familiar ring. He, too, had been at King's Cross in Sydney, when a derelict man pulled on his jacket and asked him the simple question, "If you were to die tonight, do you know where you would spend eternity?" The man giving the testimony went on to say that that question haunted him for several days and eventually drove him to his knees, and motivated him to give his life over to Jesus Christ.

A couple of years later, the minister, himself, was in Sydney. He went down to King's Cross on the outside chance that he might find that derelict man. He stood on the corner scanning the faces of the people around him, and he felt someone tug on his jacket. When he turned, there was a man who obviously was poor and ragged. Before the man could say a word, the pastor raised his hand to silence him and said, "I know what you're going to say. You're going to ask, if I was to die tonight, where would I spend eternity?"

The old derelict was amazed and asked how the pastor knew that. The pastor told him about the two men who had given testimonies at his church, and how they had become Christians because of the haunting question that *he* had raised when they visited his city. The man was reduced to tears and said, "Mister, some eight years ago I was an old drunk. But then I gave my life to Jesus. I'm uneducated. I don't know how to say much or do much. The only thing I could think of was to go around and ask people this same question over and over again. I've been doing it for eight years, mister, and today was the first day I had any idea I was doing any good at all."

Jesus doesn't expect us to be polished, or to possess the best techniques. What He does expect is that we faithfully do what we can to tell people of their need for Christ and His salvation.

That's Crazy

I was sitting at a table with a group of very sophisticated intellectuals. As our conversation progressed, they began to really rag on evangelical Christianity. At one particular point, I had had enough and decided that I had to speak out against them. I said, "You guys have got the wrong idea! You judge evangelicals on the basis of some stupid displays of zeal. For instance, at every Super Bowl game there's some crazy guy in the stands who holds up a big sign citing some Bible verse. He expects that somebody will look up that verse, fall under conviction, and be saved. You think that's what we're all like, and you judge us by that kind of stupidity."

When I finished my rabid declaration, one of the men at the table took the pipe he was smoking out of his mouth, set it down, and said,

↝　The apostle Paul once said that the love of God constrained him to preach the gospel. In short, he just couldn't stop talking about Christ, no matter how much he tried.

A little boy came home from Sunday school and told his family that the Sunday school teacher must be Jesus' grandmother. He explained that she spent a whole hour just talking about how wonderful He was and showing them a lot of pictures of Him.

Isn't it strange that most of us who are grandparents are far more ready to talk about our grandchildren than to speak a word on behalf of our Savior?

"Interesting you should mention that. Three years ago I was watching the Super Bowl. It was just before halftime when the Cowboys kicked an extra point. Behind the goal post was that man that you were talking about. He held up a sign that read, 'John 1:12.' I didn't have anything else to do during halftime, so I reached up on the bookshelf of the den, pulled off my old Bible, and opened it to John 1:12, just out of curiosity. When I opened it, there were some old notes from a Bible talk I had heard at summer camp many, many years ago when I was a teenager. I read over those notes and remembered what I had forgotten and forsaken. I got down on my knees, there and then, and gave my life back to Jesus."

What could I say? My ridiculing of that crazy man's witnessing had received just condemnation.

The Foolishness of Preaching

My wife and I were returning from New Zealand after a preaching mission, and we stopped in Honolulu to take a break from the long trip. We got off the plane with plans to catch another one on to Los Angeles some five hours later. In the meantime, we headed into the city and took a walk along Waikiki Beach. As we strolled along, we came upon a very strange looking man standing with a Bible in one hand and waving his finger at every passerby with the other. He was barefoot and wearing a dirty T-shirt and tattered trousers. To everyone who passed he pronounced the judgment of God on those who would not accept Christ.

As we passed him I said to my wife, "It's guys like that who are an embarrassment to the Kingdom of God. People look at weirdos like that and get turned off to the gospel. Guys like that leave me a bit disgusted."

An hour or so later we were heading back to catch the bus to the airport, and we came upon this same man. To my surprise, there were two very normal-looking, properly dressed men standing with him. He had his arms around their shoulders, and as I passed I could hear that they were saying a prayer, surrendering their lives to Christ. My wife looked at me and simply asked, "Well? How many people did you lead to Jesus today?"

Witnessing is an obligation. And though we may seem foolish to others, it is through "the foolishness of preaching," says the apostle Paul, that the gospel gets out into the world.

The Need to Tell the Story

The Great Commandment

A friend of mine said that we ought not to try to fulfill the Great Commission until we have first begun to live out the Great Commandment. What he meant was that witnessing for Christ requires that we have a lifestyle of love to support our claims that Jesus makes us into people like Himself. Saint Francis of Assisi once said, "We should preach the gospel all day long—and if necessary, use words!"

It's obvious that the kind of people we are and the way in which we live must back up our witness, but we cannot wait until we're perfect to declare the gospel. We must make the message clear as best we can, given our limitations. As important as it is to live a holy life as a witness to Christ, it is essential that we do our best to proclaim the Word of God in words, because people need to hear the story of salvation.

Missed Opportunities

Martin Niemoller, a German Lutheran bishop, was called upon to negotiate with Hitler during World War II, in the attempt to save the Church of Germany from being closed down by the Nazi dictator. Toward the end of his life, Niemoller told of a recurring dream that he had in which he saw Hitler standing before Jesus on Judgment Day. Jesus got off of His throne, put his arm around Hitler, and asked, "Adolph! Why did you do the ugly, evil things you did? Why were you so cruel?"

Hitler, with his head bent low, simply answered, "Because nobody ever told me how much You loved me."

The bishop reported that at this point in the dream he would wake up in a cold sweat, remembering that during the many, many meetings he had had with Hitler, he had never once said, "By the way, Führer, Jesus loves you! He loves you more than you'll ever know. He loved you so much that He died for you. Do you know that?"

So often we fail to bear witness, and hence lose precious opportunities to alter the course of history.

One at a Time

Winning new people to Christ is more often the result of personal one-on-one evangelism than it is the result of messages delivered by great preachers. Sometimes when I have a large audience, I take a survey by asking, "How many of you are Christians today because of hearing a great sermon?" At most, two or three hands go up.

I then ask, "How many are Christians because of hearing the gospel on a radio or TV show?" Again, there might be a hand or two raised.

Then I ask, "How many of you are Christians today because some ordinary person cared about you, loved you, and would not let you go until you gave your life to Christ?"

It's then that a sea of hands goes up. It is obvious that personal evangelism is, by far, the primary instrument for spreading the gospel.

Airplane Evangelism

The effectiveness of one-on-one witnessing became clear to me one day when I was on an airplane heading to Orlando, Florida. I was scheduled to speak at a huge outdoor festival that would bring together thousands and thousands of young people to hear the gospel. As I sat in my seat, I looked across the aisle, and saw sitting by the window in the seat opposite me one of the most attractive women I had seen in a long, long time. I don't want to sound sexist, but I have to say she was stunning.

Coming up the aisle of the airplane was a very "New York" looking guy. He was wearing a satin shirt with the top three buttons undone. This allowed us to clearly see evidence of his hairy chest covered by some golden chains. There was an arrogance to his step. It was an almost empty airplane, and I had a pretty good idea as to where he would choose to sit. And I was right! He sat next to *that* beautiful woman.

What followed was more than entertaining to watch. He did all the things that a guy like that does when he moves on a woman. When he had her thoroughly engaged in conversation, I watched her smile at him as she reached into her pocketbook and pulled out a New Testament. For the next two hours she had the Scriptures open and was explaining to him what the gospel story was all about.

The plane landed and we pulled up to the exit ramp. People stood and got their belongings out of the overhead compartments. It was then that I saw that the one-time make-out man had his head bowed and eyes closed. His new friend had her hand on his shoulder, and she was praying for him to accept Jesus as his Savior.

Taking in that scene I thought to myself, *Who am I kidding? In the end, it's that kind of evangelism, not my preaching, that does the most for spreading the message of the gospel of Christ.*

With Tears

As we preach, our attitudes must be Christlike or we will contradict our own words by the way in which we present ourselves.

The story is told of a church in a small town that got a new preacher. Everyone in the town was talking about how wonderful he was. Then the town skeptic asked one of the church deacons, "Why is this preacher so much better than the last one you had?"

The deacon answered, "The last one told us we were sinners, and that unless we repented we would all go to hell."

The skeptic asked, "And what does this new preacher say?"

"This new preacher tells us we're all sinners and unless we repent and accept Jesus, we're all going to hell," was the answer.

The skeptic just shrugged his shoulders and said, "I fail to see any difference between the two."

And the deacon answered, "The new preacher says it with tears in his eyes."

How Come?

Too often we are guilty of "being ashamed of the gospel of Christ." We're embarrassed about bearing witness for fear that we might be violating the rules of social propriety.

Our failure to talk about Jesus cheats some of our friends out of the blessings that knowing Him can bring. This became very clear to me when I attended the ten-year reunion of my high-school class. It was fun to see so many of my old friends whom I hadn't seen for years. Then one of my friends pulled me aside. He had been one of my closest buddies in high school. We had played basketball together and always sat together at lunch. He told me that a year earlier he had had "the most fantastic experience" of his life. He had become a Christian! He explained the change that had come over him and the new joy that he had experienced because of being in a relationship with Christ. He went on and on and on about his life as a new Christian.

After his first pause, I interrupted him and said, "Jerry, I'm so glad to hear this. You know, I'm a Christian too!"

Jerry asked, "When did you become a Christian?" I explained to him that I supposed it was when I was a little boy.

To this he responded with a most intense question. "If you were a Christian when we were in high school together, how come you never told me about Jesus? How come you never introduced me to Christ?"

I didn't know what to say.

Billy

Many years ago, when I was a young pastor, I was asked to be a counselor at a junior-high camp. Everyone should be a counselor at a junior-high camp—ONCE! For any Roman Catholics who may be reading this, I have to say that I now believe there is a purgatory. I have been there. It's junior-high camp!

Junior-high boys have a strange and often cruel sense of humor. There's a strong tendency for them to pick on some unfortunate, off-beat kid and ridicule him, making him the brunt of their jokes. This was certainly the case during this particular week of summer camp. They picked on a thirteen-year-old kid named Billy, who couldn't walk right or talk right. He dragged his body across the campground in spastic fashion, and when he spoke his words were markedly slurred.

The boys at the camp would often mimic his gestures, and they thought that was funny. One day I heard him asking for directions. I can even now hear his almost indiscernible, painfully spoken words: "Which . . . way . . . is . . . the craft shop?"

The boy he asked, mocking his slurred speech and using convoluted hand language said, "It's over—there . . . Billy boy."

But the cruelest thing they did was on a Thursday morning. Billy's cabin had been assigned to lead morning devotions, and his cabin mates all voted for him to be the speaker. They wanted to get him up there in front of everybody so they could be entertained by his struggling attempts to say anything at all.

When I found out about it, I was furious, but there was nothing I could do. It did not seem to bother Billy! Somehow he dragged himself up to the rostrum as waves of snickers flowed over the audience. It took Billy almost half a minute to say, "Je—sus . . . loves . . . me . . . and . . . I . . . love Je—sus."

When he finished, there was stunned silence. When I looked over my shoulder I saw that all over the place there were junior-high boys with tears streaming down their cheeks. Some of them had their heads bowed. A revival broke out!

We had done many things that week to try to reach the boys with the gospel message, but nothing had worked. We had even brought in baseball players whose batting averages had gone up since they started praying, but it had had no effect. It wasn't until a spastic kid named Billy simply declared his love for Christ that everything changed.

> ∕ I heard about a man who paraded up and down the streets in Philadelphia carrying a sandwich-board sign over his shoulders. On one side it read, "I am a fool for Christ." People approaching him had condescending sneers on their faces, but as they passed you would see the sneers quickly wiped away as they looked back and read the other side: "Whose fool are you?"

I travel a great deal, and it is surprising how often I come upon people who say something like, "You probably don't remember me. I became a Christian at a junior-high camp where you were a counselor. And do you know what the turning point was for me?"

I don't have to ask. I always know what I'm going to hear. "Billy!"

God doesn't need superstars to declare His Word. He loves to take "the stones which the builders reject" to use as the foundation rock for building His Kingdom.

Without Question

When I was teaching at the University of Pennsylvania I had two students who were heading to Cornell University to do graduate work. This was back in the sixties, when Marxism was in high gear at the university. One of the students, who was by far the most brilliant student I had ever had, was a thoroughgoing Marxist. The other young man, who was of average intelligence, was a young Christian and a member of a Bible study group I led each week. When I heard that they were going to room together, I was somewhat dismayed because I knew my Marxist student could outargue my Christian student on any given subject. I wondered how long it would be before the Marxist argued the Christian out of his faith.

When I met up with these two students several months later, I was surprised to learn that the Marxist had become a Christian. Out of curiosity I asked, "How did this happen? I was worried that you would *both* end up as Marxists after a couple of months."

"Every night I would argue with this guy," said the former Marxist. "I would explain to him how all of his assumptions were ungrounded. I would point out to him the validity of my political ideology. Every night we would argue, and every night I would win the argument. But he always ended our discussions with these same words: 'Mark, you overpowered me with your arguments once again, but you didn't convince me that you're right. You can't convince me that you're right! And you can't because I *know* Jesus is real. I feel Him in my life! I sense His presence every day! I have a personal relationship with Him that cannot be questioned.'"

In the end, a solid personal relationship with Christ is the strongest witness we can bear for the Kingdom.

Overhearing What God Wants to Do in the World

With any reading of the Bible, we realize that Christianity is a commitment to a God who is at work in the world. Our God wants to change this world into the kind of place it was meant to be when it was created. It will be a world marked by justice and well-being for all. In the Scriptures, this world is referred to as "the Kingdom of God." Jesus came to declare this kingdom and promised that it would be a society without poverty, racism, sexism, militarism, or environmental degradation. In creating the Kingdom of God, Christ calls upon all of us to participate with Him. He saves us from our sin, invades us with His Spirit, and empowers us with His vision. To the end of building the Kingdom, Jesus calls us to be His partners.

Recruiting

When I was young, I heard a preacher say that God wanted us to be revolutionaries, and that it was God's call that we should join up together to transform the world. This excited me. Growing up in a family with a very limited income, and sensing the injustices my father had to endure in the workplace, I was somewhat angry with the way things were in the American socioeconomic system. Living in West Philadelphia, I saw the plight of African-Americans and the impact of racial discrimination. I wanted to change the world so that such evils would not exist. And so, the call of this preacher was exceedingly attractive. This preacher was a recruiting sergeant for Jesus.

I heeded the call of that recruiting sergeant and asked what my assignment would be in this revolutionary army being called together by God. I was told that I, too, was to be a recruiting sergeant. So I went to work recruiting people. But the people I recruited were also assigned to be recruiting sergeants. And so it continued that recruiting sergeants were recruiting more recruiting sergeants, who in turn recruited more recruiting sergeants. And I began to ask myself, When do we recruit people who will do battle with the enemy? When do we fight against the principalities and powers of our age?

Little by little I came to realize that this particular brand of Christianity was an army of recruiting sergeants that recruited recruiting sergeants, not an army ready to do battle with the forces of evil or to create a new social order.

> Dietrich Bonhoeffer tells the story of a madman who drives his automobile in a reckless manner and hurts people. Eventually the man drives up on the sidewalk of the city and starts running down pedestrians indiscriminately. Bonhoeffer says that it's not enough to minister to those who are victims of the madman. The madman himself must be stopped.
>
> It was in this context that Bonhoeffer committed himself to join others in a plot to kill Hitler during World War II. He tried to stop the madman, but the plot failed. He was arrested, sent to a prison camp, and eventually died there as a martyr.

Changing the System

Christians do an excellent job of being Good Samaritans. Whenever the social system grinds out casualties, the church is more than ready to pick up those casualties, patch up their wounds, and send them back to take their place in the system once again. But it does very little to try to change the system itself.

The story of the Good Samaritan describes a good man who rescues someone who, while traveling on the road between Jericho and Jerusalem, falls among thieves. We all know the story of how the man is battered and beaten and left for dead, and how the Good Samaritan comes and picks him up and cleanses his wounds and takes him to a place where he can be cared for and nurtured back to health. It's a moving story and inspires us all to do good works.

The thing we must bear in mind is that the Good Samaritan did the right thing when he picked up the bandits' victim, but if every day two or three people get mugged on the road between Jerusalem and Jericho, there comes a point at which we must realize that being Good Samaritans is not enough. At some point, if such crimes abound, we have to figure out how to put up a better lighting system on the road and perhaps have it patrolled by police, and put an end to people being mugged on that dangerous highway. In short, it's one thing to care for the casualties from the system, but sooner or later we have to change the system so as to not have so many casualties in the first place.

It has been said that the church is God's ambulance squad. We're good at that sort of thing. But sooner or later we have to do more than just help those who fall victim to the abuses of an unjust and oppressive society. Sooner or later, there comes a point at which the call of God is to change the system itself.

First Aid

In a make-believe story set in an American city during World War II, a program was organized to train volunteers in the skills of emergency first aid. There was a fear that if the city should be bombed there would not be adequate medical care available for the people who would be wounded. There was one woman in the class who seemed bored and detached from all that was being taught. She was there out of a sense of obligation but had no enthusiasm for learning.

One day, this particular woman showed up to the first-aid class abounding with enthusiasm. She could hardly contain herself as she told the others in the class the source of her newfound excitement for the course. She said, "This class never meant much to me until yesterday! Yesterday, I was sitting on my front porch, when there was a horrendous automobile accident right in front of my house. The cars not only smashed into each other head-on, but bodies were thrown through the air. Everywhere there were people who were seriously injured. I saw blood everywhere I looked. The scene was horrible. It was so horrible I almost fainted. Then I remembered what I had learned in this class—and I put my head between my legs and I didn't pass out!"

It's obvious the woman had missed the point. She was not supposed to learn first aid simply to take care of herself, but to be equipped to take care of others. On the other hand, many of us do not realize that the reason we are nurtured in the Christian faith is not just so we can handle the stresses and the strains of our own personal lives, but that we might be ready to meet the needs of others who suffer around us.

Ending Racism

The Hillbilly Preacher

In changing the world, one of the primary problems to address is that of racism. Christ has called us to be one people and to overcome the racial differences that have separated us in the past. A story about Clarence Jordan, the founder of Koinonia Farms, gives a brilliant example of how true Christianity can overcome racism.

Clarence was the preacher for revival services at a Baptist church in the hills of South Carolina. It was in the late '50s and racism was rampant in the area, with incredible animosity between blacks and whites. In this social context, Clarence was amazed when he walked onto the platform to take his seat behind the pulpit, looked over the congregation, and saw that it was a racially integrated group. Black and white people were sitting next to one another all over the auditorium. Following the service, he had a conversation with the old hillbilly preacher who was the pastor of the congregation.

"How did you get this way?" asked Clarence.

"What way?" responded the old preacher.

"Integrated!" Clarence answered. "You know what I mean! You've got black and white people worshiping together at your church. That's really unusual down here in South Carolina. For that matter, it's unusual anywhere. Has this come about since the decision?"

"What decision?" the pastor inquired.

"The Supreme Court decision," answered Clarence. "You know! The decision that brought about racial integration of the schools and set in motion all the changes for new race relations."

"What's the Supreme Court got to do with Christians?" the preacher asked.

The old preacher's question was a good one. Christians shouldn't have to be told by any court or government legislation that they should be one with their brothers and sisters of other races.

Clarence smiled and said, "Now you know you've got an unusual situation here. Come on, now! Tell me how you got this way."

The pastor smiled sheepishly and said, "Well, this church was down to a handful when the last preacher died. It was such a small congregation, they couldn't get a new preacher nohow. They went on for a couple of months without anybody to give any sermons, so one Sunday I said to the head of the deacons that if they couldn't get a preacher, I'd be willing to preach. So he let me! When I got in the pulpit, I just opened the Bible and put my finger down. It landed on that verse where Paul tells us that in Christ there is neither Jew nor Greek, bond nor free, male nor female. And so I preached about how Jesus makes us one and how once we're in Christ, there should be no racial divisions between us. When the service was over, the deacons took me in the back room and they told me that they didn't want to hear that kind of preaching no more."

Clarence asked, "What did you do then?"

The old preacher answered, "I FIRED them deacons!"

"How come they didn't fire you?" asked Clarence.

"Well, they never hired me," the old preacher responded. (I suppose that lends some credulity to the case that paid preachers are much more vulnerable than unpaid preachers when they act prophetically.) "Once I found out what bothered them people, I preached the same message every Sunday. It didn't take much time before I had that church preached down to four!" Sometimes revival begins not when we get new people into the church, but when some of the old members leave.

"After that," the preacher continued, "we only let people into this church if they were *really* Christians. We figured you're not really a Christian until you get rid of all that racist garbage. Down here, from when you're knee high to a grasshopper, you're told about the differences between the white people and the black people, and how the races shouldn't mix. But when people are really converted and filled with Jesus, all of that kind of nonsense is washed away!"

That night, Clarence was driven to his hotel by a sophisticated young English professor from the University of South Carolina. This man drove seventy miles each way to attend this church. Clarence was intrigued by that, so he asked this young intellectual, "Why do you go to that church? You're a student of the English language, and that old hillbilly preacher can't utter a sentence without making a grammatical error. Why would you travel all this distance just to hear him?"

Clarence pretty much knew what the answer would be. He was just testing the professor. The man straightened himself out in his seat and said, with a degree of sternness, "Sir! I go to that church because that man preaches the *gospel!*"

Ebony and Ivory

The urban missionary program I helped to develop in Philadelphia and Camden, New Jersey, has had hundreds of young college students come during their summer vacations and volunteer their services.

They work with boys and girls all day long doing Bible study, playing games, providing cultural enrichment programs, tutoring, and giving the kind of personal counsel that at-risk city kids need.

One summer, a blonde-haired, blue-eyed, ethnically Dutch student from Calvin College came to join our summer outreach. She became intensely involved with a group of some fifteen African-American children who lived in one of the most dilapidated government housing projects of the city.

Toward the end of the summer, she taught the children the song called "Ebony and Ivory." It's a song about piano keys, and it makes the point that you can't make good music with just the ivory keys; you need the black keys too. The reverse is also true. You can't make much good music with just the black keys; you need white ones as well.

After she finished teaching the song, she decided to explain the point of it all to the children and she said, "What I'm trying to tell you is that you're black and I'm white, and together . . ."

The children interrupted her, objecting to what she was saying. "But you're not white!" they shouted at her. "You're not white!" they said over and over again.

The young woman was taken back by this reaction and asked, "Well, if I'm not white, what do you think I am?"

"You're light-skinned!" was the answer.

You can understand what had happened in the minds of those little children. They had come to think of white-skinned people in almost demonic terms, and here was a woman who broke through their stereotypes. In their minds she couldn't be white, because she was too good and too loving for that. They were about to learn that Christ can make people one and get them to overcome racial differences that would divide them.

We Are All Family

Peter Arnett, the one-time CNN television commentator and reporter, has had experiences that make him a fascinating storyteller.

One day I asked him, "Have you got any good stories to tell me? I live by stories and I'm running out of them."

Peter said, "I've got a wonderful story to tell you! I was in Israel, in a small town on the West Bank, when an explosion went off. Bodies were blown through the air. Everywhere I looked there were signs of death and destruction. The screams of the wounded seemed to be coming from every direction. A man came running up to me holding a bloodied little girl in his arms. He pleaded with me and said 'Mister, I can't get her to a hospital! The Israeli troops have sealed off the area. No one can get in or out, but you're press. You can get through. Please, mister! Help me get her to a hospital. Please! If you don't help me, she's going to die!'"

Peter told me how he put them in his car, got through the sealed area, and rushed to the hospital in Jerusalem. The whole time he was hurtling down the road to the city, the man was pleading from the backseat, calling out to him, "Can you go faster, mister? Can you go faster? I'm losing her . . . I'm losing her!"

When they finally got to the hospital, the girl was rushed to the operating room. Then the two men retreated to the waiting area and sat on the bench. Peter told me how they just sat there in silence, too exhausted to even talk.

After a short while the doctor came out of the operating room and said to them solemnly, "She's dead."

The man collapsed in tears, and as Peter put his arms around the man to comfort him he said, "I don't know what to say. I can't imagine what you must be going through. I've never lost a child."

The man looked at Peter in a startled manner and said, "Oh, mister! That Palestinian girl was not my daughter. I'm an Israeli settler. That Palestinian is not my child. But, mister . . . There comes a time when each of us must realize that every child, regardless of that child's background, is a daughter or a son. There must come a time when we realize that we are all family."

When I heard that story, I saw all the more clearly why Jesus came into the world. He came to break down the partitions that we have constructed that separate us into different groups. He came to make us one family.

What We Learn about Economic Justice

There are those who do not fully grasp that there can be no social justice without economic justice. There are people who are oppressed by economic arrangements that deny them fair salaries for their labors. There are economic systems that generate massive unemployment and leave them without any jobs at all. There are people who find few economic alternatives available to them and feel themselves powerless as they try to find ways to care for their families and for themselves. As Jesus works through us to establish His Kingdom "on earth, as it is in heaven," He expects us to address the tragedies that come from economic oppression.

He Will Be with Us

Some years ago, I took some of my students to a despicable slum area on the edge of Santo Domingo in the Dominican Republic. We went to attend morning mass at a Catholic church pastored by a priest whom we greatly admired because of the incredible good he had done for the people of that barrio. His compassion for the needy seemed to have no limits.

This particular morning the church was packed. My students and I stood against the back wall as we watched the mass unfold. So many people had gathered for the morning service that there were at least a hundred outside the church building, pressed against the open windows, hoping to hear what was going on inside.

The reason for the huge turnout was that the priest was reporting to the people about what had transpired in his negotiations with government officials that past week. The slum area had been slated to be bulldozed to make way for a marina so that tourists would have a place to park their yachts. This meant that the thousands of people who lived in the slum would lose their shacks, and there was no place for them to go. Each Thursday, the priest had had a meeting with government leaders at the presidential palace, with the hope of persuading them either to forego their plans to destroy this barrio or, better still, to provide the people with some new decent place to live. That Sunday, at mass, he was reporting to the people what had come out of these discussions.

When the priest finished his report, a young man in the congregation stood and yelled out, "But, Father, what if all this talk comes to nothing? What if these negotiations lead nowhere and they come to destroy our homes? What will we do when they come with the bulldozers to level all our shacks?"

Before the priest could answer, another young man on the other side of the sanctuary stood and yelled, "If they come with the bulldozers to destroy our homes, we will fight them." Then he shouted even louder, "We will fight them to the death!"

He turned to the congregation. "Are you with me? Are you with me?!"

The congregation yelled back, "Yes! Yes! Yes! We are with you!"

In the midst of this uproar, the priest raised his arms and yelled at the top of his lungs, "SILENCE!" He went to the altar, lifted up the bread and the wine symbolizing the body and blood of Christ, and turning to the people he said, "When they come with the bulldozers to destroy our homes, and we go out to fight them, *He* will be with us too!"

After that incredible morning, my students and I had a long discussion about all of this. We concluded that while the Kingdom of God would beat swords into plowshares and bring an end to violence, there was no question that in the struggle for justice, God sides with the poor and oppressed against the strong and the powerful.

A Workable Plan

More than two decades ago, some of my students entered into a research project that addressed the simple question, How could a small group of Christians effect micro social changes in society? Specifically, we designed a plan to bring about social justice in a small country. The country we chose for our study was the Dominican Republic.

In the course of the semester we all became very enthused with the project. Then one day, one of the students said, "If this is really such a workable plan, why don't we enact it? Why don't we see what we can do about changing the Dominican Republic?"

I was almost floored by the prospect, but there was no getting away from the fact that if this was a workable plan, it *ought* to be enacted.

The first step of this so-called Christian revolutionary movement was for us to buy some stock in a large multinational corporation that we believed dominated the economy of the country. Gulf and Western owned hotels and a major resort, along with massive chunks of real estate in the eastern half of the nation. They had also bought out the Puerto Rican Sugar Company and had become the major sugar producer in that part of the country.

Each of us bought one share of stock in the company, entitling us to go to the next stockholders' meeting, which we did. During the meeting, we took turns reading from Scripture and calling Gulf and Western to economic responsibility. We asked them to address the issue of low wages for the sugar workers. We pointed out the fact that the company had led the nation to depend more and more on a single-crop economy. We complained about the failure of the company to provide education and medical services for the people in the region of the country that they dominated.

We expected to be laughed out of the place. That would set us up for the next stage, which would be a more ugly confrontation. Instead, the corporate executives of Gulf and Western were more than ready to listen!

What followed over the next several months was an array of negotiations, not only with us, but with several other organizations that were committed to improving the economic and social life of the people of the Dominican Republic. One day the vice president in charge of communications called me to say that he would be making a public announcement about a commitment the corporation had made to help the people of the Dominican Republic. As he read the press release to me, I was stunned. It outlined a plan whereby the corporation committed itself to work along with Mt. Sinai Medical Center of New York to create health services in the communities throughout the eastern half of the nation. The corporation was also committed to testing the soil, and land that could be used to produce food for the indigenous corporate population would be set aside for that purpose. The plan also involved an array of educational programs that included working with us in developing a new university to train teachers, lawyers, nurses, and engineers. There were other dimensions to this plan that were equally impressive. What was amazing was that Gulf and Western followed through on their promises. They spent a half billion dollars on these programs over the next five years and, in the process, brought about radical change in the lives of the people of that region.

Here was a case where something of the Kingdom of God was realized in history because some corporate executives were willing to respond to the biblical requisites of justice.

The Sandal Factory

I teach at Eastern College, which more than a decade ago made a commitment to initiate a program on the graduate level that would train people to go to Third World countries, as well as to the impoverished sections of American cities, with the express purpose of starting small businesses and cottage industries with the poor. This special MBA Program was specifically designed to create a new breed of missionaries who would sense that their calling was to communicate the gospel in the context of entrepreneurship. They would create employment for the poor, thus enabling them to escape from their poverty on a sustainable basis.

The students who have graduated from this program have done remarkable things around the world. Some of them have joined an evangelical mission organization called Opportunity International. Based in Oak Park, Illinois, this particular organization has generated more than a hundred thousand jobs through microenterprises in countries around the world.

I was part of such a microenterprise in the Dominican Republic. In an impoverished neighborhood in Santo Domingo, we started a tiny factory that produced sandals made out of worn-out automobile tires. With simple tools and very little training, it was possible for young people to carve out the soles for sandals from discarded tires and make them into attractive and durable footwear. The boys would then take the sandals out onto the streets of the city and sell them, providing an income for their families.

We told the younger children that if they would go out to the trash dumps and vacant lots of the city and bring us worn-out and discarded automobile tires, we would give them fifty cents for each of them. It wasn't long before we had every old and discarded automobile tire in Santo Domingo. Then we started getting a lot of *new* automobile tires, and we knew we had to make some adjustments!

When we talk about Jesus, we must make it clear that He is not just interested in our well-being in the afterlife. He is a Savior who is at work in the world today trying to save the world from what it is, and make it into a place where people can live together with dignity.

Addressing the Educational Needs of People

We are unfinished creations. God is still at work trying to bring us into the fullness of our potentialities. A primary instrument for enabling us to become all that God wants us to be is education. We must develop our gifts and expand our understanding of how we can serve our Lord.

Home Schooling

Among the affiliates of EAPE/Kingdomworks are the missionary enterprises in Camden, New Jersey, run under the auspices of UrbanPromise. These programs are headed up by one of the most promising young Christian leaders in America, Bruce Main. A couple of years ago he initiated a unique educational program that is worth replicating. Bruce selected from Camden High School some young people with horrendous academic records. Almost all of them were flunking their courses and missing more days of school than they were attending. Unfortunately, such academic records are not unusual at Camden High, where more than half of the students never finish high school at all, and a good portion of those who do get diplomas can be considered functionally illiterate. Specials on television and a major story in *Time* magazine labeled Camden as "one of the worst cities in America" and its schools were described as "disasters."

Bruce put the young people he had selected in small groups of five and arranged for them to be "home schooled." Meeting in what had once been an inner-city church building, these groups came together each morning for instruction. Their teachers were inexperienced, but by using the same home-school materials utilized by parents across the country, they were able to do an effective job of enabling these high-school students to complete their educations.

To date, not only have these students completed high school, but each and every one of them has gone on to an institution of higher education following graduation. One of them was granted a full academic scholarship to Cornell University—one of our most prestigious Ivy League schools. Don't tell me that inner-city young people can't learn! These African-American students, who had been largely written off by the white establishment, more than proved their intelligence and capabilities.

Christ has called us to create such innovative efforts to rescue young people who are falling between the cracks in an educational system that is presently overpowered by problems.

Watching Them Learn

A couple of decades ago, EAPE/Kingdomworks worked with some Dominican people in an attempt to establish a small Christian university in the city of Azua. With very limited financial resources, we recruited teachers, secured some buildings, and instituted a program that was amazingly credible.

I will never forget the first time I visited that small university. The classes were held at night because the students were in no position to give up their daytime employment to attend classes. I was with the missionary we had appointed to be our liaison to the city leaders who worked with us in this venture. When we arrived at the campus, I was intrigued to see large groups of people standing around the cinder-block buildings that housed the classes, which were even then in session. These people were standing in rapt attention and absolute silence. When I asked what was going on, I was told, "Oh, don't mind them! They're the parents of the students. Each night they come here and stand outside the classes and look in on their children studying. Watching their children learn is their favorite form of entertainment."

What I saw before me were parents admiring the work of God. The Jesus who had died on the cross for them, to provide them with salvation, was there and was saving their children from the almost certain fate of unrealized potential.

Political Activism

Within the Christian community today there is little argument about the fact that the church has a responsibility to bring about social change that incarnates the values of the Kingdom of God. The big question that arises is how to go about doing it. There are those on the one hand who hold to a politically conservative ideology and believe that it is the responsibility of the church and not the government to render the essential services that are needed by the poor and the oppressed. On the other hand, those with more liberal tendencies believe that the government is an instrument of God through which Kingdom work can be done. Conservatives believe that the way to change society is to change individuals. Those individuals will then in turn transform the social order. Liberals, on the other hand, have a tendency to work for structural change in the institutions of society, reasoning that people are victims of structures that are unjustly organized to oppress the poor and the powerless. Both sides have part of the truth. And more and more, Christians are looking for ways to bring together the best elements of both the conservative and liberal ideologies. There is a recognition that we cannot change society without changing people. And there is also the recognition that we cannot change people unless we change the society that conditions their behavior. Christians are concluding that we must work to bring people into a transforming relationship with Christ and to bring justice to society simultaneously.

> ⌒ A friend of mine once said, "The difference between a conservative and a liberal is that if someone is drowning a hundred yards offshore, the conservative will throw out fifty yards of rope and yell at the drowning man, 'We've done our part. Now you must assume some responsibility and do yours.' The liberal, on the other hand, when seeing someone drowning a hundred yards offshore, throws out two hundred yards of rope . . . then drops his end of the rope."

No Power on Earth

In seeking to change the world, we must recognize that the methods we use must be Christian. The Bible is clear about that; our weapons are not those of the world (2 Cor. 10:4). When the followers of Martin Luther King Jr. marched from Selma, Alabama, to Montgomery, in what is now considered the turning point in the Civil Rights movement, they encountered an array of deputy sheriffs and National Guardsmen who were determined to turn them back. When these defenders of "law and justice" encountered the civil-rights marchers on the bridge outside of Selma, the demonstrators were told to turn back. They responded by saying, "We've come too far to turn back now!"

The demonstrators got down on their knees and bowed their heads in prayer, making themselves incredibly vulnerable. At the count of ten the order was given for the deputy sheriffs and the National Guardsmen to charge in among them and drive them back.

On live television we all watched as the demonstrators were hit with billy clubs and stung with electric cattle prods. People were beaten and dogs were released on them. It was a wild attack on citizens. As I watched that scene in which peaceful demonstrators were battered and beaten, my soul cried out, "They've won! Those civil-rights demonstrators have won!"

If you asked how a group of people being battered and beaten had won, I would have to say, God's people have a nasty habit of rising again! There is no power on earth that can keep them down.

We change the world through nonviolence and loving sacrifice, and we believe that, in the end, the gates of hell cannot prevail against us.

One Man

There is a price to be paid as you struggle to change the world, and sometimes people are called upon to pay the ultimate price.

The story is told of a monk from southern France who went to Rome to take in the splendors of the Holy City. When he arrived, he was caught up in the crowd going to the Coliseum. He wasn't aware of all that was involved in the entertainment of the day, but he soon realized what was going to happen when the gladiators took their places on the field. They drew their weapons, waved them at Caesar, then called out, "We who are about to die salute thee!"

The young monk realized that the gladiators were about to fight each other to the death, and he called out amidst the roaring crowd, "STOP! STOP! In the name of Jesus, STOP!"

His voice could not be heard above the roar of the crowd. He rushed down the aisle to the barrier that separated the cheering crowd from the strutting gladiators and again yelled out, "In the name of Jesus, STOP!" Still no one noticed him nor heard his plea.

He jumped over the barrier and ran out onto the middle of the Coliseum floor. He stood between two of the gladiators and yelled at each of them, "In the name of Jesus, STOP!"

The two gladiators ignored his words. Instead, each took his sword and ran it through the body of the pleading monk. As the man of God dropped to the ground, dead, silence fell over the crowd. Then in the stunned stillness, one man in one of the back rows left his seat, came down an aisle of the Coliseum, and left. Another followed. Then another. And another. Then still another!

> ～ Henry David Thoreau was put in jail because of his opposition to America's involvement in the Mexican War. One of his friends came to visit him and looking through the bars asked, "Henry, what are you doing *in* there?"
>
> Thoreau responded, "I have to ask you, what are you doing *out* there?"
>
> Sometimes being arrested for the cause of justice is required of Kingdom people.

As the Coliseum emptied, Caesar himself stood and left.

From that day on, there would be no more gladiator fights in Rome's Coliseum. An end to the brutality and the death all took place because one man was willing to pay the price and give his life.

What Does It Cost?

A friend of mine became a professor at a state university located near Eastern College. He invited me to speak to his students on the subject of "Christianity As a Movement for Social Change." The lecture went extremely well. I could sense that I was swaying the audience and that

I might even come away from the lecture with some converts. My friend, who was not a Christian, also sensed the mood of the crowd and became increasingly agitated. Finally he yelled out, "Before we go any further, Tony, maybe you ought to tell them what it will cost them if they join up in this cause of yours. Maybe you ought to tell them the price that goes with the kind of radical Christianity you're promoting!"

He was right! It is all too easy to talk about the glorious vision of the Christian faith and never spell out what it will cost those who choose to become agents of social change in a society that has a commitment to the status quo.

Paying the Price

A man I know went to Princeton Seminary many years ago to hear the great Toyhitiko Kagawa deliver a sermon. Kagawa was a Japanese Christian who had risked his life time and time again during World War II in order to save American airmen who had been shot down over Japan. He hid them and did his best to keep them alive by sharing his limited supply of food. It wasn't that he sided with the American cause; it was just that his Christianity compelled him to love even those who were bombing and killing his friends and relatives. In giving himself to this ministry, he was eventually caught and tortured. While imprisoned he contracted tuberculosis.

As he spoke before the students, his body was frail and his voice was weak. Sitting next to my friend at the lecture were two seminarians who seemed to be unimpressed by Kagawa's testimony. At the end of the message one turned to the other and said, "He really didn't say very much—did he?"

At that point an elderly woman sitting in front of them turned and said, "Young man! When a man is hanging on a cross, he doesn't have to say anything at all!"

Unless we are willing to pay the price, we cannot be part of the Kingdom. But those who do pay the price have credibility and deserve to be heard.

The Right to Be Heard

When I first started doing missionary work in the Dominican Republic, I linked up with a young Christian doctor named Elias Santana. Elias was a man who was ready to pay the price of building the Kingdom of God. He had turned his back on what could have been a lucrative medical practice in Chicago and returned to his native Santo Domingo to work among the poor. Whatever money he made taking care of people who could afford to pay him was spent on pharmaceutical supplies to be given away to the impoverished people who lived in the slums of his city. Day in and day out he worked among the poorest of the poor, giving them the medical help they could never have afforded. He even gave away what limited money he had.

One day, I was with Elias when he drove his truck into one of the worst slums of the city. For the next several hours he diagnosed people, prescribed cures, and did the best he could to help those in desperate need. After hours of medical work, he honked the horn of the truck, climbed on its roof, and began to preach the gospel.

As I stood in the crowd, I noticed a young man I had met previously at the state university. He was one of the prime movers for the Marxist student movement on campus. I went over and chided him, saying, "Hey, Pedro! Elias has the ear of the people. You'd better watch out! He's going to win them all to Christ, and there will be none of them left to follow you."

The young man turned to me with not a trace of a smile on his face. He said sternly, "What am I supposed to say?" Then pointing to my friend he added, "Elias Santana has earned the right to be heard."

Metropolitan Kyril

One of the most amazing stories to come out of World War II concerns a church leader in Bulgaria named Metropolitan Kyril. When the Nazis rounded up the Jews in his city and herded them into a barbed-wire enclosure, he decided to act.

The train that was supposed to take the Jews to Auschwitz pulled up at the station. The S.S. guards were just about ready to load the Jews into the box cars that would take them to the gas chambers when suddenly, out of the darkness, Metropolitan Kyril appeared. He was a tall man to start with, but as an Orthodox priest, he wore a miter on his head, which must have made him appear like a giant as he emerged out of the darkness. He was wearing his black robes and his white beard hung over them. Marching behind him were many of the townspeople.

> Those who do not believe that the world needs to be changed should go to a place like Calcutta. There's a strong likelihood that if you go there, you will meet crippled children begging for money. If that is not sufficiently horrible, consider this: Some of them have been made into cripples by their parents. Their parents deliberately break their arms and legs because they know that cripples can collect more money from the tourists when they beg than children who are whole.
>
> Obviously, such a world needs to be changed.

Kyril went to the entrance of the barbed-wire enclosure, which was then surrounded by his supporters. When the Nazi guards tried to stop him, he laughed at them and pushed aside their guns. He went in among the Jews and as they surrounded him, crying hysterically, he raised his hands. He quoted one verse of Scripture, and with that verse he contributed significantly to the changing of the destiny of a nation. Quoting from the Book of Ruth he declared to his Jewish friends, "Whither thou goest, I will go. Your people will be my people, and your God will be my God!"

The Jews cheered and the Christians joined in cheering. They were no longer separate peoples. They had become one in the declaration of the Word of God.

Because of such heroics, not a single Bulgarian Jew ever died in a Nazi concentration camp during World War II, in spite of the fact that Bulgaria was one of the Nazi powers. When a man is willing to lay down his life to oppose oppression and injustice, amazing things can happen.

Too Much Suffering

Our missionary organization, EAPE/Kingdomworks, was running special summer programs in a government housing project called Bartram Village. One summer, following the morning program, a ten-year-old boy rushed home to his apartment on the third floor of one of the housing units. When he opened the door of the apartment, he saw a man beating his mother, trying to get her welfare check. The intruder wanted to use the money to buy drugs to nurse his crack habit. His mother was screaming for help! The boy ran to the window and shouted to our missionary volunteers on the street below. They, in turn, called the police.

It seemed like only a minute or two before the cops were there. They charged up the steps into the apartment. The man, who was a two-time loser, knew that he was in for a long time in jail if he was arrested. Discounting the cost, he jumped out the window of that third-floor apartment. What happened next was horrible! He landed on a laundry pole, which went through his entire body. Incredibly, the man did not die instantly, but convulsed on the pole for ten to twenty seconds. The children, who had just been part of our ministry program, gathered around and watched the man die.

What was mind-boggling to our missionary volunteers was that the children did not seem to be bothered by it at all. They had seen too much suffering and too much death to be shocked by even such a hideous scene.

Don't tell me that such a world does not have to be changed. In the name of Christ, we must create decent housing, restore broken families to wholeness, and create a society in which children can grow up without suffering and death marking their days.

8

What We Overhear about the Family

To me, it is absolutely amazing that a book written two thousand years ago should have such relevance to the institution of the family as it exists in our modern capitalistic society. Anyone who reads through the New Testament will be amazed at how its message spells out patterns for interpersonal relationships within the context of the family, as well as presenting a strong case for a Christian feminism and a wholesome perspective on child rearing.

Love and Romance

Skin Deep

American society has glorified romance and made it the basis for marriage. There is nothing wrong with romance; it is an extremely potent force in driving people into matrimony. But in today's world, it has become the *primary* factor in the creation of marriages. Romance is highly conditional on physical appearances. The object of romantic love excites and entices a person. This means that there is often a shallowness about romantic relationships, but because the emotions are so overpowering, people sometimes don't realize what they're getting into until it's too late.

The superficiality of romance is articulated very well by a woman I know who was abandoned by her husband for another woman. When I asked if the other woman was younger, she said, "Of course he left me for a younger woman. Anybody his own age would be able to see right through him!"

Be Careful Little Hands

The day I got married I was incredibly romantic, because my sexual energy level was so high. My Baptist upbringing had caused me to be very committed to not having sexual intercourse prior to marriage. My indoctrination about sex started back in my days in primary classes in Sunday school. We used to sing a song:

> Be careful, little hands, what you do,
> Be careful, little hands, what you do,
> God is up above,
> He is looking down in love,
> So be careful, little hands, what you do!

Sometimes, when I'm speaking to a group of young people, I tell them that this particular chorus ruined my dating life. Every time I would be ready to make a move on a girl during my high-school days, I would hear those words: "Be careful, little hands, what you do . . ."

When Romance Wears Down

(This is especially for the unmarried males who are reading this.)

In our society, it is easy to get swept up in the mythology of romance. Most young people are sure that they will live happily ever after if they just marry "the right one." When they ask their mothers, "How will I *know* when I've met the right one?" the answer is always the same, "When you meet the right one—you'll *know!*" As you can imagine, an answer like that doesn't help very much.

The problems don't end there. Three weeks before the wedding, your mother is bound to ask you, "Are you sure?" It's too late then.

The wedding invitations are already out and the presents are coming in. Without any question, you're dead meat.

On the day of the wedding, in all likelihood, you'll look up the aisle and see this woman dressed in white—whom on this occasion you hardly recognize. She'll be wearing a veil so you won't be able to see her whole face. You may see what appears to be a threatening smile aimed at you. And you will be asking the question, "God? What am I doing here?" Even if you are an atheist, at that moment God will speak to you. You'll probably hear a voice saying, "Too late, sucker!"

It really doesn't make much difference, because all a wedding does is to create the *possibility* for a marriage. Marriage is what you create after the wedding is over. It's something you have to decide to create. You wake up one morning and look across the bed. She won't be awake yet. Her mouth will be open and her hair will be hanging down over her face. Worse than that, she will wake up first and look across the bed, and in your case, there may be *no* hair hanging down over your face. And romance takes a nose dive! That is when people can too easily split up.

> ↪ A teacher received an essay on Benjamin Franklin from an eight-year-old boy in her class, and it went like this: "Benjamin Franklin was born in Boston, but he did not like it there! He got on a boat and went to Philadelphia and he got off the boat. He walked up the street and he bought a loaf of bread. Then he met a lady and he discovered electricity."

When I asked a friend of mine whether he and his wife had ever thought of divorce as the romance wound down, he answered, "Of course not. My wife and I have never considered divorce. Murder, sometimes—but never divorce!"

Marriage

Just Like Mom

It has been said by neo-Freudian psychologists that a young woman looks for a partner who embodies traits that are like her father's. Maybe that's why mothers cry at weddings.

On the other hand, there's the story of a young man who could not seem to date any girls who pleased his mother. No matter whom he dated, his mother always objected or found some serious fault in her. The mother didn't like any of the girls he brought home to be introduced to her. Then one day he brought home a girl who was just like his mother. Needless to say, his mother liked her very, very much. There was only one problem—his father didn't like her!

A Very Good Day

To make a marriage work requires commitment. In the context of commitment over many years, a husband and wife can grow a marriage into something that makes romance seem frivolous by comparison.

Years ago, I was invited to speak to a group of students at Bryn Mawr College, an elitist women's school in suburban Philadelphia. I was asked to defend traditional marriage against the criticism brought by feminist ideologists.

At the end of the lecture there was a time for questions and answers and I soon found myself besieged by tough interrogators. I felt I was losing the arguments and being overwhelmed by my adversaries. Then I suddenly remembered a story that a friend of mine, Dale Moody, a former professor of New Testament at Southern Baptist Theological Seminary, had related to me about the death of his mother. It illustrated better than anything else I could have said what a loving, committed marriage is all about, and why it is superior to romance.

The day his mother died, she and Dale's father were having breakfast, when suddenly she slumped in her chair and then fell to the floor. Her husband of fifty-four years ran around to the other side of the table, swept up his bride, and went running from the house. He placed her in the front seat of the pickup truck and drove down the driveway and onto the highway like a hot rod in a race. Sadly, the elderly woman was dead on arrival at the hospital.

After they buried her, Dale, his brother, and his father retreated to the old homestead, sat on the back porch in rocking chairs, and reminisced. After an hour or so, the father asked Dale and his brother, "What do you suppose Mama is doing right now? What do you think she is doing this very moment?"

The two of them did their best to answer the question, with Dale reaching into his vast knowledge of Scripture and his wealth of theological knowledge for help. It was his brother, however, who came up with the best answer when he said, "Mom closed her eyes, and when she opened them again, the first thing she saw was the face of Jesus. I think at this very moment she's still reveling in that experience."

The old man smiled blissfully, then began to recite the words of an old gospel song: "Oh, that will be glory for me, glory for me, glory for me. When by His grace, I shall look on His face, that will be glory—be glory for me!" Then he said, "Take me back to the cemetery!"

Dale protested, "It's 10:30 at night!"

"Don't argue with somebody who has just buried his wife of fifty-four years!" responded the old man. "Now, take me back to the cemetery!"

When they got back to the grave site, the old man checked things out to make sure that everything was just as it should be. He tidied up some of the flower arrangements, rubbed some dirt off of some stones, then stood back and stared at the grave for a long, long time. He then reached out and put an arm around each of his sons' shoulders.

Squeezing his two sons against his body, he said, "Boys, it was a good fifty-four years and it ended just the way I wanted it to end—your mother went first! You see, when two people care about each other as much as your mother and I cared about each other, each wants the other to go first. I didn't want her to go through the pain of having to put me in the grave. If anybody was going to suffer, I wanted it to be me."

After a poignant silence, the old man said, "We can go home now. It was a good fifty-four years! And come to think about it, boys, it's been a good day! I hope you understand that. It's been a *very* good day."

When I finished telling the story, my opponents were dead silent. I ended the discussion by saying, "What those two elderly people had created between them over fifty-four years makes romantic infatuation and its temporary liaisons seem shallow by comparison."

And I knew I had them!

Really Looking

There are many ways in which love and romance differ, but perhaps the most significant way is in how lovers face each other. In romance, they look *at* each other, enjoying what they see. But love at its best takes place when people do not simply look *at* each other, but *into* each other, looking into the other person's eyes with the energy and dynamism the Holy Spirit provides. Empowered by God's Spirit, one person can reach down into the depths of another person's being and touch the innermost recesses of that person's soul. When that happens, one experiences the kind of love Sir Thomas More wrote about when he penned the words of his famous poem.

When More returned from warring in France, he learned that his wife's beautiful face had been devastated by smallpox. She was so ashamed of her scarred face that she did not want her husband ever to see her again for fear he would reject her. Because of this, he wrote these words:

Believe me, if all those endearing young charms,
Which I gaze on so fondly today,
Were to change by tomorrow and flee in my arms,
Like fairy gifts fading away.

Thou would still be adored, as this moment thou art,
Let thy loveliness fade as it will;
And around the dear ruin, each wish of my heart
Entwines itself verdantly still.

It is not while beauty and youth are thine own.
And thy cheeks unprofaned by a tear,
That the fervor and faith of a soul can be known,
To which time will but make thee more dear!

No, the heart that has truly loved never forgets,
But it truly loves on to the close;
As the sunflower turns on her god when he sets,
The same look which she turned when he rose.[5]

Celebrate

Without commitment, there is no love. Without commitment, sex can become exploitative and diminish the dignity of the other person. But within the context of love, and within the context of a marriage, sex takes on a whole new dimension.

I've always worried about my friends who were priests and could not know what marriage was all about. One of my Roman Catholic friends, who is a priest, loves to tell the story about the pope arriving in heaven and being told that he could have anything he wanted. The pope told Saint Peter that while on earth he was so busy administering the affairs of the Church that he never had time to study, and if it would be okay, he would like to spend some time in the celestial library just reading and catching up on theology.

A few eons later Saint Peter heard some cries from the celestial library and went down to find out what was going on. There was the pope walking up and down, wringing his hands and moaning, "I had the wrong word, I had the wrong word! The word is *celebrate!*"

We used to joke when I was a kid in Sunday school and say, "They told us sex is a dirty, filthy thing—and you should save it for the person you marry!" Unfortunately, that kind of mentality persists far too often, but within a committed marriage, sex becomes one of the most humanizing and spiritually enhancing experiences known to the human race.

Who Shall Be Least?

The sociologist Willard Waller (you wonder what kind of parents with the last name of Waller would name a kid Willard) discovered what he called the "principle of least interest." In simple language the principle boils down to this: In any relationship, whoever loves the most exercises the least power, and whoever exercises the most power is exercising the least love.

Imagine a marriage in which the husband doesn't really love his wife very much, but she loves him intensely. Now ask the question: Given that arrangement, who is able to dictate the terms of the relationship? Who calls the shots? Who holds the power? The answer is obvious. She will do anything for him, and since he doesn't care much about her, he is in a position of control.

Whenever I do a marriage seminar at a church, there is always some guy who stands up and asks, "Who's supposed to be the head of the house? That's the real question! Who's supposed to run things in the home?"

I always feel like saying, If you were a Christian, you wouldn't ask such a stupid question! A Christian never asks who's going to be the master. The Christian always asks who's going to be the servant. If you're a Christian you don't ask who's going to be number one, you ask who's going to be the last. When you ask a question like that, you're asking the same stupid question that James and John raised with the Lord when they asked, "Master, when You come into Your Kingdom, who will sit on Your right hand and who will sit on Your left?" Who will have the power? I ought to say to such a man, If you really loved your wife, you wouldn't want to dominate her with your power.

Jesus loved us so much that He was willing to give up His power and take upon Himself the form of a slave (Phil. 2). And if a man loves his wife, he should be ready to give up his power and become her servant. Conversely, the wife is instructed to be submissive to her husband. But what wife would have difficulty becoming submissive to a man that defined himself as her slave?

The ideal marriage is one in which the husband says to his wife, "Honey, my dreams, my hopes, my aspirations mean nothing to me. If I can help you to become all that you can be, I'll sacrifice everything I am for that."

In return, she says, "Oh, no! I'm ready to sacrifice my hopes and my dreams and my aspirations to enable you to become all that you can be."

And he says, "Oh, no . . ." and they have their first fight. It's the only argument that Christians are supposed to have, for the Bible tells us to outdo one another in love, with each esteeming the "other better than himself" (Phil. 2:3).

Raising Children

What Is It You Do?

I was once at a very sophisticated academic gathering at the University of Pennsylvania. I didn't want to be there, and I felt uncomfortable with the kinds of conversation that were going on. A woman colleague who taught sociology struck up a conversation with my wife and me. At one point she turned to my wife and asked, in a condescending fashion, "And what is it that *you* do, my dear?"

My wife, who is one of the most articulate people I know, shot back, "I am socializing two Homo sapiens into the dominant values of the Judeo-Christian tradition in order that they might be the instruments for the transformation of the social order into the kind of eschatological utopia that God willed from the beginning of creation!"

Then my wife asked politely and sweetly, "And what is it that *you* do?" The woman answered humbly, "I . . . I . . . teach sociology."

We must recognize that raising children is a high and holy task.

Advice

Raising children is a difficult task and people sometimes turn to the experts. But the experts are often confused and their ideas change from year to year. I once saw a sign in the window of a Washington toy store listing the different advice given to parents by specialists over past decades:

1910	Spank them
1920	Deprive them
1930	Ignore them
1940	Reason with them
1950	Love them
1960	Spank them lovingly
1970	Listen to them
1980	Put them in day care

A Happy Time

I'm an opponent of corporal punishment. People don't always agree with me. One day in class my students pressed me, and by creating hypothetical situations that were totally absurd, they forced me to admit that there *might* be circumstances in which corporal punishment would be required. But then I added, "You should never strike a child in anger!"

The following day, one of my students came into class and said to the other students, "Before the professor starts his lecture, there's a little poem I'd like to read in honor of what he had to say yesterday." He proceeded with these words:

> Never strike a child in anger.
> Never hit him when irate.
> Save it for some happy time
> When both are feeling great!

Proper Correction

Trying to figure out how to correct a child is difficult, but a brilliant story was told to me by the grandson of Mahatma Gandhi as an example of how it is *best* done.

Gandhi was born in South Africa, and after his university training, he went to India to lead the struggle against British colonialism. He had every intention of returning to South Africa to lead the struggle against apartheid, but sadly, as we all know, he was assassinated before he could do that. Gandhi's son took up his father's commitment to end apartheid, and so the family returned to South Africa to work toward that end.

His grandson Arun Ghandi told me that one day his father asked him to drive him to a meeting in Johannesburg. "My father asked me to drop off the automobile at the repair garage and then be back at five o'clock to pick him up," he said.

The grandson went on to say, "I dropped my father off for his meeting and got the car to the garage by one. Since it was a long time until five o'clock, I figured I could go to the movies, which I did. That day there was a double feature being shown, and when I got out I checked my watch and realized that it was past five o'clock!

"I rushed to the corner where my father had said he would be waiting for me, and when I saw him there, standing in the rain, I tried to think of excuses I could make. I rushed up to him and said, 'Father, you must forgive me. It is taking them longer to repair the automobile than I thought it would take, but if you wait here I will go and get the car. It should be ready by now.'

"My father bowed his head and looked downward. He stood for a long moment and then he said, 'When you were not here at our meeting time I called the garage to see why you were late. They told me that the automobile was ready at three o'clock! Now I have to give some thought as to how I have failed, so as to have a son who would lie to his own father. I will have to think about this. So I am going to walk home and use the time during my walk to meditate on this question.'"

Arun Gandhi said, "I followed my elderly father home that rainy, misty night, watching him stagger along the muddy road. I rode behind him with the headlights of the car flashing ahead of his steps. And as I watched him stumbling toward home, I beat on the steering wheel and said over and over, 'I will never lie again! I will never lie again! I will never lie again!'"

It is obvious that this was a way of correcting a child that did not involve punishing the child directly, but showed the child how much hurt a parent feels when a child does what is wrong.

9

What We Overhear about the Church

The Usher

Jesus was hard on institutionalized religion and yet He, Himself, was a very religious man. So often true religion is contradicted by the behavior of the clergy and also by what goes on in an institutionalized church.

When Mahatma Gandhi was a university student in South Africa, he decided to give Christianity a try and went to a worship service at the Anglican cathedral. While sitting in a pew in the back of the church, one of the ushers came and tapped him on the shoulder and politely told him that colored people were not allowed to worship in that particular cathedral.

Reflecting on the event, Ghandi later remarked, "That poor usher. He thought he was ushering a colored man out of a cathedral, when in reality he was ushering India out of the British empire."

For Free

Clarence Jordan, the founder of Koinonia Farms and an advocate of the simple lifestyle, was once taken on a tour of one of the most magnificent church buildings in America. The people of that church had donated huge amounts of money to build an edifice that would startle the viewer with its magnificence. As Clarence was taken to the front of the church, the tour guide pointed to a cross and commented, "That cross was donated by one of our wealthiest members. It cost over ten thousand dollars!"

Clarence responded wryly, "Shucks! Time was you could get one for *free!*"

It's easy for the church to forget its mission and to utilize huge resources for buildings to honor a Savior who told us that He did not dwell in temples made with hands.

I'd Be a Baptist

A preacher was pounding away at the pulpit, and yelled out to the congregation, "Is everybody here a Baptist?"

A man several rows back answered, "No! I'm a Methodist!"

"Why are you a Methodist?" asked the preacher.

"Well, my mother was a Methodist," said the man. "And my father was a Methodist. So they raised me as a Methodist."

"That's the dumbest thing I ever heard," said the preacher. "If your mother was an ignoramus and your father was an ignoramus, would you be an ignoramus?"

"No," said the man. "If my father was an ignoramus and my mother was an ignoramus, I suppose I'd be a Baptist."

Don't get the wrong idea, I really love being a Baptist. It's just that I don't believe we should take denominationalism

> ∽ One of the scandals of Christianity is denominationalism. That we are divided up confuses the world and is a contradiction to the will of the Christ who prayed that we might be one. Sometimes when I speak, I like to have little quips that make fun of denominationalism. I, myself, am a Baptist, and I love to joke about the rigidness of many of my fellow Baptists. One of my favorites is to ask, "What's the difference between a Baptist and a terrorist?" The answer is, "You can negotiate with a terrorist!"

too seriously. I joke about it a lot, and I joke about it with my friends. When someone asks me, "If you weren't a Baptist, what would you be?" I answer, "Ashamed!"

Light Bulbs

I hope you're not offended by these denominational barbs. I contend that true Christianity exists in all denominations, and that we must see beyond the superficial differences to the oneness we have in Christ. It's within that context that I'm able to make fun of denominations and long for the day when the ecumenical spirit will prevail.

There are a whole host of "light bulb" jokes that poke fun at denominations. For instance:

Question: How many Episcopalians does it take to change a light bulb?

Answer: CHANGE? Did you say CHANGE?

Question: How many Presbyterians does it take to change a light bulb?

Answer: Four. One to change the light bulb, and the other three to talk about how much better the old light bulb was.

Question: How many Methodists does it take to change a light bulb?

Answer: We really don't know. But we want to *affirm* your decision to change the light bulb and we want to *celebrate* your new light.

Attacks upon Christendom

He Was a Clown

Kierkegaard tells a story that raises questions about the effectiveness of the clergy in declaring the gospel. In it, he points out that because the clergy are who they are, they cannot be taken seriously.

As Kierkegaard tells it, there was once a circus, and one day there was a fire in the main tent. The fire spread to wheat fields nearby and then began to burn toward the village in the valley below. The ringmaster yelled, "Someone must tell the people about the fire! Someone must tell the people to run for their lives! Someone must go into the village and let them know that the fire is coming toward them and that the town will burn unless they do something to stop it!"

The clown, still in full costume, decided to heed the call.

> It has been said that Christianity started in Israel, then was taken to Greece and turned into a philosophy. Then it was taken to Rome where it was made into an institution. Later, it was taken to Europe where it became a culture, and then it was brought to America where it was made into a business enterprise.

He jumped on a bicycle and rode into town sounding the warning. He pedaled up and down the streets yelling at people, "Do something! Run for your lives! Stop the fire! There's a fire coming this way! Your town is going to be burned to the ground unless you do something right away!"

Unfortunately, the people just stood along the sidewalks and applauded the clown. The more he screamed, the more they applauded. The more he yelled his warnings, the more they cheered him. They didn't take him seriously. "But after all," says Kierkegaard, "he was a clown!"

Look Everybody!

A friend of mine was conversing with one of the older women of the congregation following a church service, when the minister's son ran up on the platform, stood in the pulpit, and blurted out over the loudspeaker, "Look, everybody! Look! I'm in the pulpit!"

> Kierkegaard once said, "It is one thing to love the human race so much you're willing to die on a cross to save humanity. It's quite another thing to expect to earn fifty thousand dollars a year describing a man who died on a cross to save humanity."

The elderly woman said to my friend, "His father does that every Sunday."

Being a preacher myself, I know the temptation to use the pulpit as a means of calling attention to oneself, instead of preaching the gospel.

Sometimes It's the Congregation

It's not only the clergy that can be criticized. Congregations deserve their share as well. Too often the clergy is blamed for what is wrong with the church, when in reality we have to recognize that it's also the people in the congregation who contradict Christianity. Congregations can often be the real barriers to the work of God.

We Could Use You

Imagine a moderate-sized church of 170 members. It's Sunday morning and an attractive young couple arrive and take their place in the congregation. All during the service the other church people are eyeing the couple, and when the service is over they pounce on these two new faces.

"What do you do?" they ask of the young man.

"I'm the new eighth-grade teacher down at the school, and my wife has just taken a position as a music teacher," he answers.

What follows is totally predictable. The church folks are all over the young couple trying to make them feel extra welcome. Eventually, somebody gets down to what this is really all about: "We sure hope you make this your church home, because we can really *use* you!"

The church is supposed to be a body of believers that loves people instead of trying to *use* them. Too often, people in churches feel used and even misused, instead of being cared for by God's people.

He Already Has!

The church has a mission to the world, but it often lacks the resources to carry out that mission, even though its people have the financial resources that are required.

One time I had flown into Philadelphia on a red-eye from the West Coast. When I got off the plane at 8:30 A.M. I was met by my secretary, who broke the news to me that I had a speaking engagement at ten that morning. She said, "I don't know how we missed this one. Somewhere along the line the notices of this engagement fell between the cracks. I wanted to be here to meet you because you need to be taken directly to the church. It's one of those World Day of Prayer services, and you are supposed to deliver a 'missionary' message."

When I took my place behind the pulpit I wasn't thinking clearly, and I was too tired to be any place other than in bed. Consequently, I did not react as I should have when the woman leading the meeting announced to those gathered that she had a prayer request from a missionary in Venezuela. She described a wonderful doctor who had given her life to serving the poor in the barrios of Caracas. This missionary doctor was asking for five thousand dollars to put an addition onto her medical dispensary. The addition was desperately needed because with her present facilities she wasn't able to handle all the sick and infirm who came her way.

The leader of the group then asked, "Dr. Campolo, would you please lead us in prayer that the Lord might provide the five thousand dollars that is needed by our sister in Venezuela?"

Before I could catch myself I said, "No! But what I will do is take all the money I am carrying on me and put it on the altar. And I'm going to ask everyone else here to do the same. No need to write out checks! We'll only accept cash! After we've all put the cash we're carrying on the altar, we'll count it. Then I'll ask God to write out a check for the difference."

It was a good day to pull this off, because I was only carrying $2.25. The leader smiled benevolently and said, "We've all gotten the point, haven't we?"

I responded, "No! I don't think we have! My $2.25 is on the altar. Now it's your turn!"

She was somewhat taken aback by my aggressive request, but she opened her wallet and pulled out $110 and slapped it down on top of my meager offering. Then I said, "We're on our way! We've got $112.25. Now it's your turn!"

I pointed to a woman who was sitting in the front pew over to my right. She looked around and smiled a bit. Then she got up and came to the altar and put her cash on top of ours. I got the next woman to do it, then the next, and the next. It took me more than twenty-five minutes to take up the offering as one by one, woman after woman came and placed her money on the communion table. When they had finished taking turns laying their money on the altar, we counted it. We had taken in more than eight thousand dollars. Even then, I knew I hadn't gotten all of the cash. I could see some of the women putting in meager offerings, holding back most of what they had and giving me dirty looks.

There wasn't any time left for me to preach. I don't think they wanted to hear from me anyway, so I simply said to the congregation, "The audacity of asking God for five thousand dollars, when He has already provided us with more than eight thousand dollars. We should not be asking God to supply our needs. *He already has!*"

Two Wrongs

Sometimes church people are just downright legalistic. They lose the essence of the gospel in an array of petty rules and regulations. A friend of mine, who lives next door to a Seventh-Day-Adventist woman, talked about being confronted by her on Saturday morning as he was cutting the grass on his front lawn. The woman said in an abrupt, condemning way, "It's the Sabbath! You're cutting grass on the Sabbath!"

My friend, trying to defend himself, sheepishly responded, "Well, Jesus picked corn on the Sabbath," to which the woman shot back, "Two wrongs don't make a right!"

My friend said that the worst part of it was that the woman didn't see the humor in what she had said.

He Drank Wine

Not long ago I found a newspaper article that gave an example of how we make legalism the essence of Christianity, even when it runs contrary to the teachings of Christ. The article told of a man who wanted to get a license to serve wine in his restaurant in what was a dry county of Georgia. In making his case to the county commissioners, he pointed out that Jesus drank wine when He was here on earth. One of the commissioners, who was a Baptist deacon, answered in an angry voice, "I know! And He has always been an embarrassment to me!"

I suppose that Jesus would be an embarrassment to all of us who have created a strait-jacket religion out of His freewheeling lifestyle of grace.

They Haven't

When I pastored a small church in a rural community, I discovered that a young woman of the town had become pregnant out of wedlock. The word was out, and the gossip about her condition was everywhere.

I went to see her and even as I knocked on the door, I had this uncanny awareness that the Holy Spirit was on me in a special way and that something unusual was about to happen. The young woman invited me in, and as I sat in her living room explaining the forgiveness of God and how God wills for each of us to have a new start, she responded with great intensity. She gave her life to Christ, and I watched joy cross a face that an hour before had been marked with sadness.

I wasn't surprised when she showed up at church the following Sunday. She showed up the week after that and the week after that. And then she stopped coming. I went to visit her again and asked why she wasn't attending church anymore. She said, "I can't! Every time I go into that church I get the feeling that I'm dirty and no good."

"You shouldn't feel that way," I said. "Jesus has forgiven and Jesus has forgotten."

I'll never forget her answer. She said, "Jesus may have forgiven, and Jesus may have forgotten. But the people down there at your church—they haven't forgiven. And, they haven't forgotten."

I was reminded of that verse of Scripture where the apostle Paul says of the church, "Because of you, the gospel is made of none effect."

It's Still an Assembly of God's Finest People

Negative things can be said about God's people in the church, and I have to be reminded that God isn't finished with us yet. Furthermore, I must always be aware of the goodness to be found in the church, if I only stop to look for it. The same can be said about the clergy. Some of them may be hypocrites, but for the most part I find that they are leaders worthy of the respect the Bible has instructed us to give to those who are nurturing us in the faith.

What He Was

A friend of mine joined an AIDS support group made up of people who had family members dying of this dreaded disease and who had a need to come together to find in community the emotional support that would enable them to endure what confronted them.

One woman in the group was especially negative toward the church and pointed out that she didn't go to church anymore because the people in her congregation were so condemning of her son and so judgmental of her for raising a boy who turned out to be gay. It would be fair to say that she had reached the point at which she hated the church.

In the course of her tirades, she happened to mention that the only person who had ever given her any help was an elderly man who had recently moved in next door to her. "Every morning," she said, "he comes over and has coffee with me and listens to me unburden myself. He holds my hand and comforts me as I cry. If it wasn't for him, I don't know what I would do. Why can't church people be like that?"

What the woman didn't know was that that man was a retired Presbyterian minister. He didn't tell her about his previous vocation because he knew that, more than anything else, she needed a friend who would listen. He knew that if she was aware that he was a clergyman, there might be a barrier to the love he could give. Telling her about his past life would come in due time. For the present, a shoulder to cry on was most important.

Sometimes we clergy types are not as bad as our detractors claim.

The Altar

Even when we're looking our worst, some of the good in us seems to surface. I remember a television show shortly after the time that Jim Bakker, the televangelist, had his fall into infamy because of sexual misconduct. The ministries of the PTL Club were in disarray. Everything was falling apart, and to highlight the destruction of

Bakker's kingdom there was a bankruptcy auction of all the stuff that Jim Bakker had accumulated over the years.

The sale created a media frenzy because such outlandish things as his air-conditioned doghouse were put on the auction block. But what was of special interest to me was the sale of Jim Bakker's desk. A man had flown down from Toronto, Canada, to bid on the desk, and it was obvious from the beginning of the auctioneer's request for bids that this man was going to buy this desk, no matter what. When the auctioneer's hammer slammed down and he shouted the word, "Sold!" one of the TV reporters got hold of the man and asked him why he was willing to travel so far and pay so much for Jim Bakker's desk. The man's response was memorable.

"This may look like a desk to you," the man answered. "But it's much more than that to me. You see, some five years ago my wife and I got a divorce. We had created tremendous hurt and disillusionment for each other and there was no way that the marriage could continue, so we went our separate ways. Then, about a year ago, I got a telephone call from her and she told me she was down here in North Carolina. She had just spoken to a man named Jim Bakker who had given her hope. She wanted to know if I would come down and join her because she was convinced that, if I would listen, we could get our marriage together again.

"I flew down here as quickly as I could. My wife and I sat on one side of this desk while Jim Bakker sat on the other side and explained to us the way of salvation. He told us that if we gave our lives to Christ, the past could be wiped out and we could have a whole new beginning.

"That day I accepted Jesus, as my wife had done the day before. Our marriage *was* restored, our lives were renewed, and everything changed.

"Mister!" said the man, "This may look like a desk to you, but to me it's an altar. It's the place where I committed my life to Christ. To me, it's a sacred piece of furniture, and I just couldn't stand the thought that it might fall into the hands of someone who wouldn't appreciate what it is to me."

My mother always said, "There is so much good in the worst of us, and so much bad in the best of us, that it makes no sense for any of us to criticize the rest of us."

Perspective

In the midst of the uproar following the televangelist scandals, Ted Koppel, the ABC television reporter, held a meeting at a church in Memphis, Tennessee. On the platform were assembled half a dozen of the leading televangelists in the country. Each was given an opportunity to answer questions and to defend television evangelism to the two-thousand plus people who were gathered to hear what they had to say.

Because the program was taped, Koppel was able to do something that was really quite wonderful. He had previously taped an interview with a preacher in the hills of Kentucky who served a small church. This preacher was the epitome of sincerity and had served his church well, in spite of the fact that he lacked seminary training. This interview was played just prior to the discussion with the televangelists.

The program opened with viewers approaching the church as seen from a helicopter. Viewing the church from above, we could hear them singing the invitation hymn, "Just As I Am." The cameras then took us inside the church where we saw people coming down the aisle, giving their lives over to Christ, confessing their sins, and being comforted by this loving pastor. Then we were invited to listen to the interview that Ted Koppel had with this backwoods preacher. The man had given up a job as a mailman, where he was paid thirty-six thousand dollars a year, in order to be the full-time pastor of this congregation of less than a hundred believers. For the next couple of minutes, the pastor gave us an overview of what it was like to be the minister of a small country church like his.

After the interview with this pastor we were taken into the auditorium of a large megachurch in Memphis, where most of the rest of the program unfolded. For the next three quarters of an hour, we listened as television evangelists talked about their respective ministries and the potential television had for spreading the gospel. Then, toward the end of the program, we were taken back to that little church in Kentucky. The pastor had obviously been allowed to see the video of the television evangelists describing their work, after which Koppel asked, "Well, what do you think about all of this? What do you think about these television evangelists and the millions and millions of people they are reaching through the television medium?"

The old preacher seemed dazzled by what he had just seen and heard. His response was memorable. "What those men are doing is absolutely wonderful! Imagine reaching millions and millions of people every day with the good news about Jesus. You know, Mr. Koppel, it takes all of my time and all of my energy just to take care of the ninety-six members I have in this little congregation. It takes all of my time and all of my energy just to love them and care for them day in and day out."

Ted Koppel quietly responded by saying, "I suppose it does . . . This is Ted Koppel bidding all of you listeners, goodnight!"

What I saw on that show that night has served as a reminder that alongside all the glitz and glamour of big-time ministries, most of the work of Christ's Kingdom is carried out by people who are unknown and ask for no other applause than that which comes from nail-pierced hands.

He Tipped His Hat

It was my privilege once to be on the same speaking docket as Nobel Prize winner Bishop Desmond Tutu. Before the service began, I was carrying on the small talk that people usually use to fill the time. Jokingly, I asked the bishop why he wasn't a Baptist. "After all," I said, "in this country most black people are either Baptist or Methodist." In a moving story, the bishop explained why he had become an Anglican priest.

He told me that in the days of apartheid, when a black person met a white person on the sidewalk, the black person was expected to step off the pavement into the gutter to allow the white person to pass, giving the white person this gesture of respect. "One day," the bishop told me, "when I was just a little boy, my mother and I were walking down the street when a tall white man, dressed in a black suit, came toward us. Before my mother and I could step off the sidewalk, as was expected of us, this man stepped off the sidewalk and, as my mother and I passed, tipped his hat in a gesture of respect to *her!*"

The bishop said, "I was more than surprised at what had happened and I asked my mother, 'Why did that white man do that?' My mother explained, 'He's an Anglican priest. He's a man of God, that's why he did it.'

"When she told me that he was an Anglican priest," said Bishop Tutu, "I decided there and then that I wanted to be an Anglican priest too. And what is more, I wanted to be a man of God."

Strike one up for the Anglican clergy!

One of Them

If you go to Hawaii and ask around, you're likely to hear the story of the priest who was sent to minister to the lepers who lived on an isolated island in the Hawaiian chain. The entire island had been set aside as a leper colony, and this priest had gone there to do his best to minister to the scorned and sickly people who lived there. For years he reached out to them as best he knew how to share with them the love of Christ, but he never connected with the people in a way that led them to respond to his ministry. After a long but unsuccessful period of pastoring, he decided to give up. He sent word to the people of Oahu to send a boat to take him away from the colony, and to send someone else to take his place.

On the Sunday morning when the boat was scheduled to arrive, as the priest stood waiting on the dock, he happened to look down at his hands and noticed several white spots. He suddenly realized that he, himself, had become a leper. He wouldn't be able to take the boat back to Oahu, for now he also belonged in the colony. He left the dock and slowly walked up the hill toward the little church he had tried to serve so faithfully.

When he arrived at the church some two hours later, he was amazed to find that, for the first time, the church was filled with people. They had come to hear their priest. He was no longer an outsider. He had become one of them. The priest stayed on to minister to lepers for the rest of his life and touched thousands with Christ's love in the years that followed.

Strike up a victory for a Catholic priest who followed the example of Christ and came to suffer among the people he loved.

Pope John

Sometimes we are so critical of institutionalized religion that we fail to see the goodness inherent in many who are trying to make it work. As a young man in graduate school, I became intrigued with Pope John, the pope who called Vatican II into session. What particularly pleased me about Pope John was his sense of humor. When asked by a reporter how many people worked in the Vatican, Pope John answered, "About half of them!" On another occasion, when he was being interviewed by the media, the pope was asked what he would tell the church to do today if he knew that Christ's return was to occur tomorrow. He smiled and answered, "Look busy!"

Before he became pope, he had served as a cardinal. He had been particularly effective in negotiating with the Communist leaders of Italy who, at that time, dominated the political scene. On one occasion, as he walked out of a particularly intense negotiating session, he had his arm around the leader of the Communist party and was overheard to say, "You see! I told you! The only thing that really separates us is our convictions!" What an incredible statement. Here was a leader of the Church making it clear that love unifies even those whose ideological differences should make them enemies.

On Hearing

It's so easy to be critical of the clergy. Most of us are all too ready to look for shortcomings in those who pastor the local churches to which we belong.

One summer when I was a teenager, I went off to a church Bible conference in the Pocono Mountains. The man who led the conference was a prominent evangelist from the Philadelphia area named Percy Crawford. This man preached the gospel with such clarity and effectiveness that I was caught up in his message and went down the aisle at invitation time to give my life to Christ.

When I returned home, I was armed to attack my pastor. I was ready to question him as to why he had never preached the gospel, because it was clear to me that I had never heard the gospel in his church. Why did I have to go away to a Bible conference to hear the story of salvation? Why hadn't he, in his sermons, made the salvation story clear to me? I was committed to confronting him at the first opportunity.

The next Sunday, I went to church and sat firmly in my seat and listened intently. I wanted to provide a critique for my pastor and point out what was missing in his sermon. *Would you believe that was the first Sunday I ever heard that man preach the gospel?* He did it again the next week, and then the next! And then it began to dawn on me. The fault was not his. He had been preaching the gospel all along. I just wasn't hearing it.

That's Our Job

I belong to a large African-American congregation in Philadelphia that for decades was pastored by Dr. D. W. Hoggard. When he died and the congregation sought a new pastor, I was amazed to discover that they had selected a young man who was just graduating from seminary. I couldn't believe it. I told the chairman of the deacons that a large church like ours should have somebody who was experienced. I told him that we needed somebody who was a great preacher!

The response to my inquiry taught me something about what a church can be when it is at its best. The old deacon looked at me and said, "Then we're just going to have to take this young man and make him great!"

What a wonderful attitude. The deacon was aware that a pastor's effectiveness is largely dependent upon what the people in the congregation enable him or her to be.

We Will

A pastor of a Presbyterian church told me about his early days of ministry when he served a small country church.

There was a young woman who came to his church and presented her child for baptism, a child that had been born out of wedlock. In a small rural community, a woman like that can find herself shunned.

The day of the baptism the woman stood alone before the congregation, holding her child in her arms. The pastor hadn't recognized the awkwardness of the situation. He came to that part in the baptismal service when the questions are asked, "Who stands with this child to assure the commitments and promises herewith made will be carried out? Who will be there for this child in times of need and assure that this child is brought up in the nurture and admonition of the Lord?" It was then that he realized there was no godmother or godfather on hand to answer the question. But without hesitation, as though on cue, the entire congregation stood and with one voice said, "We will!"

Those who think that church people are all bad should have been around on that Sunday, for then they would have had a chance to see the church at its best. They would have seen the church as a nurturing community.

God's Fragrance

The author Rita Snowden tells of her visit to a small town near Dover, England. She was having tea in the late afternoon when she became very aware of an unbelievably pleasant scent filling the air. She asked the waiter the source of the scent and was told that it came from the people passing by. He explained to her that they worked in a perfume factory down the street and were on their way home. When they left the factory they carried with them the fragrance that had permeated their clothes during their day's work.

Rita Snowden immediately saw this as an illustration of what the church can be like at its best. We should be a people who allow ourselves in worship to be permeated with the love of Christ and the sweetness of His presence. Then as we go forth into the world the fragrance of the Lord goes with us, and all the people we pass experience something of God's fragrance through us.

No Other Plan

There is a made-up story that describes Jesus returning to heaven after His sojourn here on earth. The angels gathered around the Lord to find out about all the things that happened on earth. Jesus explained to the angels how He lived among people, shared His teachings, expressed His love, died on the cross to atone for humanity's sins, and was resurrected to declare that the new Kingdom is at hand.

When he finished telling his story, Michael the archangel asked the Lord, "What happens now?"

Jesus answered, "I left behind a handful of faithful men and women. They will tell the story! They will express the love! They will spread the Kingdom!"

"But what if they fail?" asked Michael. "What will then be the plan?"

Jesus answered Michael by saying, "There is no other plan!"

Ours is the responsibility to be the instruments for the propagation of God's truth. That is the task of the church.

10

What We Overhear about Work

Max Weber, the famous German sociologist, once said that "Luther and Calvin did away with the monasteries and, in turn, made the whole world into a monastery." What he meant by that was that serving God is not something you do away from your worldly vocation, but in the midst of it. The reformers made it clear that the love of God must be expressed in the daily labors that go with our vocations. The Bible tells us that whatever we do, whether in word or in deed, we must do heartily as unto the Lord, and not as unto men (Col. 3:17, 23).

Nary a Ship

My wife and I visited Scotland on a speaking tour, and I had an opportunity to take her to the shipbuilding town from whence her father had come to America. Peggy wanted to see the shipyard where her grandfather had been employed, so we asked around and got directions, but we still had trouble finding the place. Finally, we asked a middle-aged woman if she could help us. She said, "Of course! I work there! I'm on my way to work right now. It's time for the evening shift."

As we walked down the hill toward the shipyard, people from the day shift were going home from work. As they passed us, each and every one of them knew the woman and wished her, "Good day." The woman seemed to know everybody, but in a town of that size that didn't surprise me. As we continued on our way, I asked her, "And what is it that you do down there at the shipyard?"

The woman stopped, which required that we stop too as we listened to her answer.

"What do I do?" she repeated. "I'm the one who shines the brass on the ships." And then with a pride that I have seldom seen on anyone's face, she went on to say, "And nary a ship goes to sea until I give approval that the brass is as it should be!"

It was obvious to me that this wasn't a job to her. This was a divine calling! The work she did had a sacred significance to it.

A few years later I read in the paper that the shipyards at Port Glasgow had been closed, and that ships would be built there no more. I immediately thought of that woman and I wondered how she handled all of that.

To take away a person's job is often to wound that person's spiritual identity.

Teddy Stallard

Elizabeth Ballard of Chesapeake, Virginia, tells the story of a schoolteacher named Miss Jean Thompson that illustrates brilliantly how work can be ministry.

Each September, Miss Thompson greeted her new students with the words, "Boys and girls, I love you all the same. I have no favorites." Of course, she wasn't being completely truthful. Teachers do have favorites, and what is worse, they sometimes have students they just don't like.

Teddy Stallard was a boy Miss Thompson just didn't like, and for good reason. He was a sullen boy who sat slouched in his seat with his head down. When she spoke to him he always answered in monosyllables of "yes" and "no." His clothes were musty and his hair unkempt. He was an unattractive boy in just about every way. Whenever she marked Teddy's papers she got a certain perverse delight out of putting Xs next to the wrong answers. And when she put the "F" at the top of his papers, she always did it with a flair. She should have known better. Teachers have records, and she had records on Teddy:

First grade: Teddy shows promise with his work and attitude, but
poor home situation.

Second grade: Teddy is a good boy, but he is too serious for a second grader. His mother is terminally ill.

Third grade: Teddy is becoming withdrawn and detached. His mother died this year. His father shows no interest.

Fourth grade: Teddy is a troubled child. He needs help.

Christmas came. The children brought presents to Miss Thompson and piled them on her desk. They crowded around to watch her open them. All the presents were wrapped in brightly colored paper, except for Teddy's present. His was wrapped in brown paper and held together with Scotch tape. But to tell the truth, she was surprised that he even brought a present.

When she tore open the paper, out fell a rhinestone bracelet with most of the stones missing and an almost-empty bottle of cheap perfume. The other children giggled at the shabby gifts, but Miss Thompson had enough sense to snap on the bracelet and take some perfume out of the almost-empty bottle and put it on her wrist. Holding her wrist up to the other children she said, "Isn't it lovely?" The other children, taking their cue from the teacher, all agreed.

At the end of the day when all the other children had left, Teddy came over to her desk and said softly, "Miss Thompson . . . All day today you smelled just like my mother used to smell. That's her bracelet you're wearing. It looks very nice on you . . . I'm really glad you like my presents." After he left, she got down on her knees and buried her head in her hands and cried and cried and cried, and she asked God to forgive her.

The next day when the children came to class, they had a new teacher. It was still Miss Thompson, but she was a new teacher. She cared in ways that the old teacher didn't. She reached out in ways that the old teacher didn't. She reached out to all the children, but especially to Teddy. She nurtured them and encouraged them and tutored them when they needed extra help. By the end of that school year Teddy had caught up with a lot of children. He was even ahead of some.

Teddy moved away and Miss Thompson didn't hear from him for a long time. Then, one day, seemingly out of nowhere, came a note:

Dear Miss Thompson,
I'm graduating from high school. I wanted you to be the first to know.

Love,
Teddy Stallard

There was no address. But, four years later there was another short note, and it read:

Dear Miss Thompson,
I wanted you to be the first to know. I'm second in my class. The university has not been easy, but I really liked it.

Love,
Teddy Stallard

And four years later there was still another note:

Dear Miss Thompson,
As of today I am Theodore J. Stallard, MD! How about that! I wanted you to be the first to know.
I'm going to be married, the 27th of July to be exact. I want you to come and I want you to sit where my mother would have sat. You're the only family I have now. Dad died last year.

Love,
Teddy Stallard

And she went. And she sat where Teddy's mother would have sat . . . because she deserved to be there. She was a teacher who had done something great for the Kingdom of God, and she deserved her reward.

The Mailman

One Friday a young professor of English literature at a state university walked into the academic dean's office and announced that he would not be back on Monday to teach. He was quitting. The dean explained that there was no way he could just walk out on his contract. If he quit, he had no future in teaching. He would be blackballed for any job for which he applied at any other school. To all of this, the young professor simply shrugged his shoulders and said, "That's okay."

His mother called me and told me what he had done. She asked me to go and talk to him. After all, if he did not teach, what else could he do with a Ph.D. in English literature? Conceding to the plea of his mother, I went to see him. He was living in an attic apartment in Trenton, New Jersey. It was one of those with-it lofts, decorated with interesting posters and bookcases full of avant-garde books.

He told me to sit down in a beanbag chair. The thing was like a giant amoeba and I felt almost devoured by it. He looked at me and he said, "I quit. That's all there is to it. I couldn't stand it anymore. Every time I walked into that classroom, I died a little bit."

I understood what he was talking about because I, myself, was a college teacher at the time. I knew what it was like to walk into a classroom and pour your heart out for truth—truth wrenched from suffering and pain, gleaned from the sorrow of human existence! And after you cry and bleed for truth, some student in the last row raises a hand and asks, "Do we have to know this for the final . . . ?" And a college professor dies a little bit.

After a while I was aware that there was no way to dissuade him from his decision. "Well, what are you doing now to make a living?" I asked.

"I'm a mailman," was his answer.

"A Ph.D. mailman. Now that's something!" I responded.

He laughed and said, "There really aren't too many of us out there."

Being raised on the Protestant ethic, I then said what you would expect me to say: "Well, if you're going to be a mailman, be the *best* mailman you can possibly be!"

"I'm a lousy mailman," he answered with a laugh. "Everybody else in my post office gets the mail delivered by two-thirty in the afternoon, or three at the latest. I never get it delivered until about five!"

"What takes you so long?" I inquired.

"I visit," he said. "You can't imagine how many people on my route never got visited until *I* became the mailman. There are interesting people on my route who are interested in literature. There are hurting people who need the comfort that comes from the great poets. There are people who read and want to share what they've learned. I can't go to sleep at night!" And when I asked him why, he said, "It's hard to go to sleep after you've drunk twenty cups of coffee."

I wasn't surprised when I found out the following year that the people of his mail route had gotten together and thrown a surprise birthday party for him at the local American Legion hall. He was special to them, and they were special to him. His mail route had become a mission field.

Work should be a way of living out our commitments and our love for people. So far as it is possible, we should settle for nothing less. Work should be a means for spiritual fulfillment.

Mixing Cement

Christopher Wren was the architect who designed some of the most magnificent churches in the world. He was the one who facilitated the construction of the great St. Paul's Cathedral in London.

While the cathedral was being built, Wren took a tour of the work site and asked the various artisans about their labors. As he left the cathedral, he saw an old man mixing cement in a mortar box, and he asked, "And what are you doing, sir?"

The man, not recognizing that it was Christopher Wren who asked the question, said proudly, "What am I doing? Why, sir, I am building a great cathedral!"

Now, there's a godly attitude toward work. That cement mixer saw what he was doing as part of a larger plan that gave his humble labors incredible significance. Would that we all could see our jobs as part of the plan of the Great Architect of the Universe, and therein find our significance too.

Risk

Sometimes we stay frozen in vocational roles that deplete us of our spiritual energies simply because we refuse to take a risk. But risk is what life is about at its best.

When I was a boy in West Philadelphia, the favorite game on our street was stickball. It was played with a broomstick and half of a tennis ball. It could be played with any number of kids and was perfect for the city streets. It was perfect, except for the fact that when we played the game we blocked traffic. That meant the police would come and chase us. We never objected to that, because it was their duty to chase us. What we did object to was that they always took our broomsticks and ended the game.

One day we wanted to play stickball, but there weren't any sticks around. They had all been "captured" and were in the back room of the police station at 55th and Pine Streets. I sat on the steps of our row house with my friends and said, "Somebody ought to sneak in that back room at the police station and steal back some of our sticks." One of the guys looked at me and said, "I dare you!"

Where I come from, to refuse a dare is to be labeled "chicken." So I said, "Okay. I'll do it, but I need your help. You guys go into the police station and keep the cops occupied. Talk to them! Pretend you have to do a term paper or something! Ask them questions! Keep them talking to you. And while they're talking to you, I will sneak along the floor and I will get in that back room, and I will come out with five sticks . . . or I won't . . . come out . . . at all!"

They did what they said they would do, and I did what I

promised I would do. While they had the cops engaged, I sneaked into that back room and got five sticks, then I sneaked back toward the door.

To this day, the name Tony Campolo is legend on the streets of West Philadelphia! I'm the guy who robbed the police station!

The excitement of risk is not to be compared to much else in life. To laugh is to risk appearing foolish. To weep is to risk appearing sentimental. To reach out for another is to risk rejection. To expose your feelings is to risk revealing your true self. To place your ideas before others is to risk ridicule. To love is to risk not being loved in return. To live is to risk dying. To hope is to risk despair. To try is to risk failure. But risk must be taken, because the greatest hazard in life is to risk nothing at all.

All of this is to say that emotional emptiness and psychological discontent in your job may require that you risk everything and dare to do that which you are inwardly called to do by the Spirit of God.

Wasted Dreams

I took a group of students to see some of the work our mission agency was doing in Haiti. We were up in the northern part of the country, where we have a medical clinic, and we saw three hundred plus people, all desperately ill, lined up for help. There was only one doctor and two nurses, and they could only take care of about sixty or seventy folks. The rest were turned away. It was fairly obvious that a significant number of them would never come back. They were too sick to make the trip another time. One of my students, Charlie, looked on all of this and said, "Doc! I'm going to be a doctor. I'm going to come back here and be a doctor! Wait and see! I'm going to go back to school, finish my work, and go on to medical college. I'm going to be a missionary doctor in this place. Just you wait and see!"

Well, I met Charlie in New York a few years later. I bumped into him on the sidewalk and we talked. After we exchanged pleasantries,

I discovered, to his credit, that he had become a doctor. But do you know what he was doing? Cosmetic surgery. And, not doing the kind that makes any sense. He was doing the kind of cosmetic surgery that caters to a sexist culture that evaluates women by the shape of their breasts.

The more he talked, the more I felt a queasiness in my stomach. He told me how he was still going to church and making financial contributions to the ministries of his congregation. He went on and on until I couldn't handle it any more.

"Stop! Stop it!" I said to him. "Just stop it! I don't want to hear any more. Charlie, you had dreams! You had visions! You were going to do something incredibly significant with your life. And look at you, Charlie! You sold out the dreams. You sold out the visions! For what? A Jacuzzi and a Porsche, that's what. You have a brilliant mind. A young man with skills and you sold out to the system, and for all the good things the system can give you. Dress it up any way you want, Charlie. You're a sellout! Do you hear me?"

A couple of years later I told that story in a Lutheran church in Southern California. In the congregation there was a young man who had a nervous disorder, and about every forty-five seconds he would make a disturbing moaning sound. He disrupted my concentration. It became increasingly difficult for me to continue my talk. I was inclined to ask him to leave, but then I thought better of it, and did my best to finish my sermon. Afterward, I retreated back to the hotel where I was staying, despondent that the evening had been such a failure.

Two weeks later, I received a letter in the mail from a woman in that church. She told me that that particular young man seldom comes to church because of his malady. But he came that particular night because he had read some of my books and really liked me. He was sure I wouldn't mind. (That made me feel all the worse.)

Her letter went on to explain that the following Sunday he came to her Sunday school class of young adults and asked for the opportunity to speak. He did his best to communicate amidst the moaning and groaning created by his disorder. He related the story of Charlie, as I had told it, and he concluded by saying, "I can't ever be a doctor because of what I am. I can never go to the mission field like Charlie could have. But if I could . . . if I could . . . I wouldn't waste my life, like Charlie is wasting his."

By the end of the class time, five of the young men and women there had committed their lives to missionary service.

Good Business

When it comes to choosing vocations and using them for the glory of God, I have some prime examples.

Some lawyers in West Virginia who heard me speak about the needs of the poor decided to set aside one tenth of their time and all of their legal resources to help people who could not pay for them. Hundreds of people who needed help came their way. What was most interesting was that they ended up prospering beyond anybody's imagination. Word of their generosity got out and brought them all kinds of additional business. Beyond that, there was the fact that people who had owed them fee payments started sending in their checks. They did not have to go after those who owed them money; it just came pouring in. What they did they did out of love for others, but it certainly benefited them in the end.

In Pittsburgh, Pennsylvania, some Christian doctors got together and opened up offices in the basement of a church. There, they make their services available to the poor without charge. What is even more interesting is that the churches around Pittsburgh have publicized what they're doing, and clients who are well-off go to the clinic and pay to have their medical needs met. It's interesting to go there and to see upper-middle-class people sitting next to poor folks from the ghetto in the waiting room. The doctors tell me that it does wealthy people a lot of good to rub shoulders with the poor, to talk with them and find out what their lives are all about. Those who can afford to pay do so, and those who can't get their services for free. This has enabled these doctors not only to stay in business, but to make the ministry of their church powerfully relevant to the neighborhood.

In Philadelphia there is a policeman who is known in the government housing project where he serves as Officer Harris. He chose to be in this community as a policeman because he wanted to be involved in the lives of the boys and girls who lived there. He participates in tutoring programs and recreational programs, and has made his policeman's beat a place of ministry. He claims that he has more contact with people in need than most ministers ever experience. I'm sure he does.

What People Need

I often serve as a motivational speaker for corporate gatherings. One time I was at a sales conference for one of America's largest insurance corporations. The speaker before me was amazing. His topic was, "How to Sell Insurance to People Who Don't Need It!" His speech was brilliant, his delivery was excellent, and he held his audience in the palm of his hand. You could see that by following his instructions anyone could get people to buy insurance, regardless of how much coverage they already had. He talked about how to play on people's fears and anxieties, how to manipulate people and set them up so they would sign on for insurance before they realized they didn't need what they were buying. His suggestions for psychological manipulation were a wonder.

When he was finished it was my turn to speak, and my opening line was a simple and direct statement. I said, "Everything you've just heard is wrong!"

Needless to say, a shock wave ran through the audience. But I went on to explain to these salespeople that they were among the few in America who had the rare privilege of actually selling something that people really need. "People *need* life insurance," I told them. "Why would you degrade yourself by selling insurance to people who already have enough of it when there are so many people who don't have what they need? People should not be manipulated! People should not be set up just so you can make a few extra bucks at their expense! People are sacred and should be treated with the utmost respect. Manipulating them to buy what they don't need is not worthy of you!"

I went on to tell the group about a friend of mine who found out that Martin Luther King Jr. had no life insurance. My friend followed Dr. King for two weeks until he cornered him in a hotel room and finally persuaded him to secure a million-dollar life policy. Less than a year later, Martin Luther King Jr. was blown away by an assassin's bullet, and after the fanfare died down, all his family had left was that insurance policy.

My friend had met a need, and he had great comfort in knowing that he had helped a family. That's what all of our labor should be about. It should be about helping people. We should be able to offer up our labors as service unto God. The president of the company was the first to his feet to give me a standing ovation.

But Don't Forget to Have Fun Too!

Two Things Are True

Because work is seen as a divine calling, too many of us are caught up in a work ethic that makes us driven people. There are too many of us who have to be working to have any sense of value at all. There is a drivenness that pervades our personalities.

I love to tell the story of that Presbyterian elder who was so into work that even his vacation time was work. Can't you see him waking up his children at six in the morning and shouting, "Wake up! Wake up! It's vacation time!"

As the bleary-eyed family members line up to get into the automobile, he admonishes them, "When you get into that car, two things will be true: the gasoline tank will be *full* . . . and your bladders will be *empty!* And we will drive and drive and drive until two things are true: the gasoline tank will be *empty* . . . and only then will your bladders be allowed to be *full!* Should your bladders become full before the gasoline tank is empty . . . may God have mercy on you!"

The Ant and the Grasshopper

As a boy growing up, I was often told the story about the ant and the grasshopper. My teachers at school explained to me that during the summertime the grasshopper just played and played and never stored anything up for the wintertime. The ant, on the other hand, worked diligently day and night. When the winter came, the ant had enough to eat and he survived the winter, whereas the grasshopper died as soon as winter came.

> ꝰ The tendency to make fun into work is all too evident in our culture. Sören Kierkegaard once described a man who was assigned the responsibility of having fun all day long. But the man was so efficient, he was finished by noon!

This was supposed to be a sufficient warning that we should work constantly and not take time to play around. But one of the boys in my fifth-grade class raised his hand and said, "But isn't it true that the ant also died? And he died without having lived at all!"

I need to listen to that fifth-grade boy. All work and no play not only makes Johnny a dull boy, but it also is an un-Christian attitude toward work.

11

What We Overhear about Ourselves

The Bible tells us that we are significant. As incredible as it may seem, the great God of the universe loved us so much that He gave Himself for us. That's the heart of the Christian message. No one should ever say, "I'm insignificant." You are so important, contends Saint Augustine, that if you were the only person who ever lived, Jesus would have died on the cross, *just for you!*

Spelling Baseball

Children start off with a sense of significance. But their feelings about being wonderful and special are often beaten out of them in the process of socialization. I remember how, as a boy in sixth grade, I learned an important lesson about what the system can do to a little boy to make him feel like nothing.

I always walked to school with my best friend, Albert. Albert was brilliant! Without question, he was the smartest kid in the class. I was proud to be his friend.

One day, at the start of the school day, our teacher announced that we would be playing a game. I was thrilled with that prospect! Then she said we would be playing "spelling baseball"!

I didn't know how to react. I loved baseball and I hated spelling. When it came to playing baseball, I was the best in the class. But when it came to spelling, I was among the worst. As an Italian kid, the English language never made much sense to me. Any language that spelled pneumonia with a *p* seemed crazy. Talk about spelling baseball had me really confused.

The teacher chose captains. Albert was one of the captains and Mary was the other one. Every class has a Mary. She was one of those perfect little girls with ribbons and bows and patent-leather shoes. If the class was required to hand in a book report, hers would be covered with special colored paper with drawings and beautiful lettering all over it. The teacher would then hold up her book report and say, "Isn't Mary wonderful? Look how beautiful her work is!" Down deep inside, most of us really didn't like Mary because she was just too special to be liked.

Albert and Mary took turns choosing up sides. I figured that if Albert was my friend he'd choose me first. But to my surprise, he didn't! I waved my hand at him, so as to call attention to the fact that I was there. But he looked right through me and kept on choosing others. It was then that I realized that in this game friendship meant nothing. The only thing that mattered was whether or not one could be successful in the competition.

The selections went on and on, but no one chose me. Finally, there were only two of us left. The other kid was a recent immigrant who hadn't yet learned English at all. Finally, the teacher *assigned* me to Albert's team. Neither Mary nor Albert wanted me.

You probably know how this game is played. Each team member is asked to spell a word, and with each correct spelling that team has an imaginary player who advances a base.

I blew it on "grasshopper"! I didn't realize that grasshopper had two

> ⁓ Don't ever call yourself a loser. Consider the fact that you were once a sperm! You were once with a group of more than five million other sperm. Then all five million of you lined up at the starting line. And at the end of a long, long tunnel there was one egg. There was a race! And you WON!
>
> Don't ever call yourself a loser. The odds were five million to one against you, and you came through. You're a winner! You make the Olympics seem insignificant by comparison. You are here by divine appointment. You are here because God chose you to be a winner in the struggle for existence.

ps. No one is lonelier than the first one out in spelling baseball. As I crawled to my seat, the members of the opposite team cheered my failure. And what was worse, the members of my own team booed me!

As I sat there with my ego decimated, the teacher turned to the opposing team and asked, "Does anyone on this team know how to spell "grasshopper"? Mary knew! Not only did she know *how* to spell it, but she spelled it with a flair. I can still hear her saying with aplomb, "Grasshopper. G-R-A-S-S-H-O-P-P-E-R." With each letter I felt pain. It was like a knife going in me every time little Mary sounded out one of the letters. She did it with such style—her shoulders swaying back and forth with each enunciated letter. If Lesson #1 was that success was more important than friendship, Lesson #2 was that Mary's success was built on my failure.

Why do we set kids against each other like that? Why do we make them enemies and diminish their sense of worth—all in the name of a game that's supposed to help them to be better spellers?

The good news of the gospel is that there is a Jesus who is proud of each of us and calls each of us by name. I don't think Jesus carries a wallet. But if He does, I am convinced that your photograph is in it. You are that special to Him. And no put-down in the world can change that.

Taking My Picture

A friend of mine told me a wonderful story about his four-year-old daughter. There was a thunderstorm and he was concerned that she might be frightened by it, so he rushed upstairs to her bedroom to check on how she was doing. Lightning was flashing and thunder was roaring outside. But when he got to her bedroom and looked in, he saw his daughter standing on the windowsill, leaning spread-eagle against the glass.

"What are you doing?" he shouted at her. "Jennifer, what are you doing?"

The little girl responded, "I think God is trying to take my picture!"

Now, there's a kid who knows how special she is in the eyes of God.

Yellow

When my son, Bart, was just a little guy, he had a favorite blanket. He actually gave the thing a name. It was called "Yellow."

Bart needed Yellow every time he was upset or tired. Just pressing Yellow to his little face brought him instantaneous comfort and the assurance that all was well with the world. He used the blanket so often and demanded it so constantly, that we ended up tearing the blanket in half. That way we could give him one half while we washed the other.

The blanket disintegrated. It became like a rag. But no other blanket would do when Bart was upset. On one occasion I can remember driving home late at night with Bart asleep in the backseat, moaning and groaning. I said to my wife, "Give him Yellow." She responded with a degree of shock, saying something like, "The last thing I told you when we left the house was to pick up Yellow. Didn't you do it?" Don't get the wrong idea. We weren't about to have an argument because this was a time for us to close ranks in support of a troubled kid.

If you saw old Yellow you would consider it worthless, but to us that blanket had great value. Its value was established, not intrinsically, but because someone we cared about loved it very much. And so it is with you. Your value is established, not because you are a great achiever, but because you have intrinsic worth. You are valuable because God loves you. We can never diminish a person's worth, for the King of Glory loves that person infinitely.

God Establishes Our Identity

If people in today's world are suffering from an identity crisis, it is only because they are not in a right relationship with God. God tells us who we are and what our lives are about.

Who Am I?

At the end of World War II, there were more than fifty men who came out of prison camps in Indochina suffering from amnesia. They couldn't remember who they were, and there were no records to help identify them. Then someone came up with the idea to run their photographs in a Parisian newspaper and announce that these men would make an appearance on the stage of the city's Opera House. The plea went out that if anyone thought they might know any of these soldiers, they should come to the Opera House and make the identification.

According to the story, on the appointed evening, the first of the soldiers marched onto the stage and looked out over the audience. As the spotlight focused on him, he asked, "Does anybody out there know who I am?"

What a question! How often

> ↶ The question is often raised as to why the righteous suffer while some of the really evil people of this world prosper. I love the response of Mother Teresa who once said: "God! You would have more friends, if You treated the few that You do have a little better."

do people ask it quietly, within themselves. The only way to answer that question is to come to your Maker. For only your Maker knows who you are and what your life is supposed to be about. God knows because, as your Maker, God knows who you were designed to be.

Lose Yourself

As a college professor, I could always count on someone coming into my office around the beginning of May and telling me he wasn't coming back next semester. (It was usually a guy.)

I would try to be professional and ask, "Pray tell! Why?"

The student would look at me and say, "I need time!" If I asked why he needed time, the answer was invariably, "I need time to find myself!"

There's a whole generation of students out there trying to find themselves. And they're all looking in the same place—Boulder, Colorado!

You could predict any one of them saying something like this: "Doc, I'm tired of playing the roles that others have prescribed for me! I'm tired of being the person my family expects me to be, that my friends expect me to be, that this school expects me to be, that the church expects me to be! I've got to peel away each of these socially prescribed identities and the socially generated personas. I've got to peel them away one by one and come to grips with the core of my being—the essence of my selfhood!"

When I hear that kind of stuff, I get a bit queasy in my stomach, and I cannot help but say in return, "Charley! What if, after you peel away each of these socially prescribed identities and socially generated selves, you discover you're an *onion!* What if you take that long guru journey into yourself, and when you get there—*nobody's home?* Stop to consider the fact that if you peel away all the layers of an onion, guess what you have left? Nothing! And it just may be that when you take that trip to the innermost recesses of your soul, that's exactly what you'll find."

I am convinced that the self is not an essence waiting to be discovered through philosophical introspection. Quite the contrary! I believe that the self is an essence waiting to be created! We create who

> ~ Sometimes, people's only commitment is to their individual well-being and ego gratification. Consider the story of a man who went into a church in Florence, Italy, and saw an old woman on her knees worshiping a painting of the Virgin Mary. Impressed by the woman's devotion to the mother of Jesus, the visitor commented about her to the priest.
>
> "Oh, don't be impressed by what you see," said the priest. "Many years ago, that woman modeled for the artist who painted that picture. What she's really worshiping is herself."
>
> No more needs to be said!

we are through the commitments we make. And without commitments we have no identity. That's why Jesus said, "Whosoever seeks to find himself, will lose himself. But, whosoever is willing to lose himself, for my sake and the sake of my Kingdom, will find himself."

Jesus is telling us that it is in commitments to Him and the work that He has for us to do that we discover who we are and what our lives are all about.

There Come Times of Questioning and Doubt

Who we are and what our lives are about are often called into question by things that go on in our own lives and in the lives of those around us. Doubt and confusion overtake even the most committed Christians.

Some Explaining to Do

When Mother Teresa visited Haiti, she was shown one of the most horrendous slums in the world. She was asked, "How do you explain all of this in light of our claims that our God is a loving God? Why does God let things like this happen?" Mother Teresa answered, "When I see Him, He's got a lot of explaining to do!"

I jokingly say that this is probably why she lived so long. Every time she approached death, I imagine God saying, "Hold up! Don't let her die yet! I don't think I can handle her right now."

He Was There

William Sloane Coffin, one-time chaplain at Yale University, lost his son in an accident. At the funeral, the minister conducting the ceremony made some feeble statement about the accident and the boy's death being God's will. Before he could finish, William Sloane Coffin stood up and yelled at the preacher. "The hell it was! It wasn't God's will at all. When my son died, God was the first one who cried!"

We always ask the question, "Where is God?" when troubles come our way. Like William Sloane Coffin, Martin Luther also lost a son. His wife, Katie, shouted at him, "Where was God when our son died?"

Martin Luther answered, "The same place He was when His Son died. He was there watching and weeping!"

At the End of the Rope

Whenever anyone escaped from Auschwitz, the Nazi prison camp in Poland, the S.S. troopers would arbitrarily choose six people to be hung. It was their way of discouraging people from trying to escape. Any prisoner contemplating escape knew that if he got away, six innocent people would die.

After one escape, a twelve-year-old boy was among those chosen for the torturous death. When the trapdoor of the scaffold swung open and the boy fell, his body weight was too light to snap his neck and kill him. Instead, the boy hung from the rope squirming and shaking for almost half an hour until he slowly choked to death. As he hung there, shaking in the cold of the evening, one man asked another, "Where is God? Where is God while all of this is happening?"

> ↶ Hendrik Kraemer, the bishop and leader of the church in Denmark, described the panic that overtook the clergy of his diocese as the Nazis marched in to take possession of their country. The clergy came to his house and asked, "What should we do?"
>
> He answered, "First, we must ask who we are! If we know who we are, then we will know what to do."

The man he asked pointed to the boy at the end of the rope and said, "He is there. God is right there."

12

What We Overhear about Our Cultures

The Book of Revelation tells us that the dominant culture is "Babylon." In the Bible, Babylon represents a society that is seductive, luring people into idolatry, materialism, and self-indulgence. Those of us who study sociology know that there are such tendencies in contemporary American society, and that the church must struggle against them, day in and day out. This chapter is about that struggle, and what Christians must do to keep from being conformed to this world.

In Our Image

George Bernard Shaw once said that, "God created us in His image and we decided to return the favor." This process of creating God in our own image so as to have God represent the dominant values of the culture is known as *totemism*. It was explored in detail by Emil Durkheim, the classic French sociologist, in his book *The Elementary Forms of Religious Life*.

This totemistic tendency was evident to me when I visited a Chinese Catholic church in Philadelphia. In the front of the church there was a stained-glass window, and you can imagine what I saw. There was Jesus; but instead of Jesus looking Jewish, He was very Chinese. The people of that church had recreated Him in their own image.

In a Sunday school class in an African-American church, the famous print of Salamon's head of Christ was removed one day from the wall. In its place there was a new picture of Jesus, in which Jesus was portrayed as a black man. When the teacher commented that

Jesus was not African-American, one of the young men in the class mumbled back, "He wasn't any honky either!"

That young man didn't want Jesus made into a white man any more than white people want Jesus made into a black man. Each group wants a Jesus that deifies themselves. But in the end, such religion is nothing more than a group worshiping a collective representation of themselves.

Totemism is what Paul was talking about in the first chapter of Romans when he describes the process whereby people take the image of the incorruptible God and transform Him into an image likened unto corruptible man (v. 23). Is it any wonder that the Ten Commandments tell us that we should make no graven images unto God? That is because any image we make of God is more of an expression of what we are like than it is of what God is like.

Who Cares?

The culture not only seduces us into idolatry, it also seduces us into materialism. Being Christian means struggling against mammon.

When I was teaching at the University of Pennsylvania back in the 1960s, I had a huge number of students in my course on the Introduction to Sociology. One day, as I was trying to wax eloquent, one of the students, dressed in army khakis and showing off a head of very long hair, stood up and shouted at me, "Bull*xxxx!*"

I shot back, "That's no way to talk to me. Now sit down! And, if you don't sit down, I'm going to toss you out of this class!"

The young man responded arrogantly, shouting back at me, "Who cares!?"

I retaliated by saying, "If I throw you out of this class, fella, I'm not letting you back in. You're finished for this course!"

Again he yelled, "Who cares?!"

I didn't push him. This was the '60s. I can just imagine where it would have gone if I said that if he was thrown out of the course he'd probably flunk. He probably would have said, "Who cares?" And if I had told him that if he flunked the course he would probably get kicked out of school, I have a feeling he would have yelled, "Who cares?!" And if I had told him that if he got thrown out of school he probably wouldn't be able to get a job, he would have shouted once more, "Who cares?!" And if I had told him that without a job he wouldn't be able to buy all the things this society tells us we have to have, he would have shouted back loud and clear, "WHO CARES?!"

I suppose that until a Christian is able to shout "Who cares?" with conviction about all that society tries to sell, that person will find it difficult to be a true disciple of our Lord.

The Wrong Prices

In the city of Philadelphia, the night before Halloween is always designated Mischief Night. You can imagine what bad little boys do on that particular evening.

Two of us broke into a five-and-dime not far from my house. We didn't steal anything. We did something far worse. We went around and changed the price tags on just about everything in the store. The next morning, people found that radios were selling for ten cents apiece, while bobby pins were priced at ten dollars. What was valuable had been made cheap, and what was cheap had been made valuable.

That story is indicative of what has happened to America. It is almost as though someone has broken into our society and changed the price tags. We are not willing to invest very much in what is really precious, and we seem to spend all of our time and energies on that which is worthless. Our values are all mixed up!

In Its Place

The media have an incredibly seductive influence on the culture. All teenagers are impacted by what they see on television. Robert Pittman, the founder and chairman of MTV, once said, "At MTV, we don't aim for fourteen-year-olds; we *own* them!"

Babylon employs technology to serve its purposes. Some argue that technology is neutral and can be used for either good or evil. But sociologists such as Jacques Ellul have contended that its overarching effect has been to enhance humanity's belief that with technology it can conquer anything, and therefore does not need divine intervention. Thus, so far as Ellul was concerned, technology nurtures idolatry in that it encourages us to think of ourselves in godlike fashion.

Some years ago I took some of my students from Eastern College into the Pennsylvania Dutch country to interview an Amish bishop. This was an incredible privilege because the Amish are reluctant to allow anyone to interview them about their lifestyle. This bishop, however, had become a friend and gave us this rare opportunity.

As we sat together and talked, the bishop explained that the Amish were not opposed to technology, but just felt that people ought to know what technology would do to them and to their way of life before they accepted it. He pointed out that over the years the Amish had observed that most technology had impacted the American people in negative and even disastrous ways. As a case in point, he cited television. He asked the students whether they would have to agree that television had taken over the place of parents in giving children values and in determining their beliefs about right and wrong. Then he inquired as to whether or not they thought that was a good thing. He contended that after watching the effects of television over several decades, many people would conclude that its influence had been somewhat ungodly, and that the American people would be better off without it. But by then it was too late to get it out of our lives.

The Amish bishop went on to explain that technology could be useful if it was not allowed to invade our lives. To emphasize this he pointed down to the end of the long lane that led up to his farmhouse. He called attention to a telephone booth that he had the telephone company install at that spot. He said, "I like to have a telephone available for an emergency. It's a good thing to use when you need to call for help or make connections with people outside of our family of friends and relatives. But why would you want a telephone inside the house?" he asked. "Telephones intrude into the most precious moments of life. You may be talking to your children or sharing something important with your wife; if the phone rings, you will allow it to interrupt what you're saying. The family can be at prayer, and if the phone rings you will stop and answer it. You could be with your wife in bed, and you will allow the ringing telephone to interrupt what you are doing there!"

He went on to say that electricity could be a good thing, if kept in its proper place. One proper place for it was in the barn. There, electricity could be used to maintain refrigeration for milk. But he went on to say that when you bring electricity into the house, it has horrendous effects. He talked about how electricity disrupts the natural rhythm of life. "People stay up later than they should," said the bishop, "and it's not long before people have radios in their houses and, through radios, become more involved in the outside world than they are with the Amish world."

When asked about tractors, the bishop pointed out that to plant and harvest with horse-drawn farm equipment requires the whole family to be involved in the work. Tractors, he explained, provided a solitary way of plowing and harvesting. He saw advantages in his wife and children working along with him in the fields, hour by hour, day by day. That, he contended, is one of the ways in which family solidarity is created.

By the end of the interview, I could see that the Amish way of life did not seem quite as ridiculous to my modern students as it had just a few hours earlier. They were now well aware that technology had changed their way of life, and they were doing a lot of reflecting on whether or not it had created a lifestyle that was good for them and good for the Kingdom of God.

Nothing to Say

Picking up this theme of questioning technology within our culture, it seems appropriate to talk about how Henry David Thoreau reacted when he discovered that Americans were utilizing a new invention called the telegraph.

As workmen were stringing wires through a meadow close to Walden, Thoreau went over to investigate and inquire as to what was happening. The men putting up the telegraph lines explained that there was this new invention. One of them said, "Haven't you heard? With the telegraph, the people in Maine can communicate with the people in Florida."

Thoreau responded in a whimsical manner, asking, "But what if the people in Maine have nothing to say to the people in Florida?"

There you have it! In our modern world of mass communication we are able to connect with each other instantaneously, only to find that we have nothing significant to say. Cable television has made it possible for us to choose from hundreds of programs at any given moment. But the shallowness of the content of the shows on those many channels makes us aware that we have improved the means of communication, but we have very little worth communicating.

Cultures Will Be Restored

According to Scripture, cultures were created by God, and in the end, cultures will be purged of their evil content and lifted up to glorify their Creator. The word "nations" really comes from the Greek word *ethnos,* which means "ethnic cultures." What the Bible clearly suggests is that on that great day when God shall gather the nations around the throne to worship our Savior, we will have an array of ethnic groups, each offering praises in its own unique ways.

Year 2000

On the New Year's Eve that brought in the year 2000 we got a glimpse of the glory and wonder of ethnic diversity. As the hours passed and moved toward midnight we were given, via television, glimpses of how different people around the world celebrated the dawn of the new year. We saw magnificent dances from the South Sea Islands and from African villages. We had the privilege of hearing from the various capitols of the world, each providing a taste of its own indigenous music.

As I watched it all, I thought to myself that heaven will be a wonderful place, because all the ethnic groups of the world will bring their songs to the throne of grace. Each will enjoy the splendor of the worship of God in diverse ways, according to the culturally defined ways of worship provided by the manifold ethnic groups gathered there.

Welcome

More than a decade ago I was on a speaking tour in New Zealand. I found that John Perkins, the prominent African-American Christian leader in community development, had been there a month earlier and had caused quite a stir. As he was pleading for respect for the indigenous Maori culture before an important gathering of church leaders, he was confronted by a man who tried to make the claim that there was no way that Christians could respect the Maori culture because it was permeated by demonic influences. The man made the claim that demon worship was so much a part of the Maori culture that, as Christians, they should destroy it.

John Perkins responded brilliantly. "Perhaps you're right. It may be that the Maori culture is permeated by demonic influences and needs to be purged. But before we try to purge the Maori culture of its demonic influences, perhaps we should first try to purge the white man's culture of *its* demonic influences."

His answer was inspired. It reiterated the message that Jesus communicated so clearly when He called upon people to not look for the splinters in the eyes of others until they had first gotten rid of the beams in their own eyes.

New Zealand is a small country and its people are very connected.

By the time I arrived there, word of Perkins's encounter had spread from one end of the country to the other. It was not long after my arrival that some Maori Christians asked me what I thought about his remarks. I let them know in no uncertain terms that I agreed with them. I went on to explain that I believed that the Maori culture was created by God and that while some evil influences had permeated it, as it had all cultures, God basically loved the Maori way of life and wanted to purify it and lift it up to what it was originally intended to be. I explained that the more Christianized the Maori society became, the more "Maori" it would be. The music, dances, and other art forms of the Maori people should not be rejected, but should be utilized as instruments for glorifying God. It is hard to describe the enthusiasm with which my Maori friends greeted my perspective on their culture, and I was soon to see its impact.

Two days later, I was speaking at a youth rally on the South Island. The word had gotten down there that I viewed the Maori dances as an instrument of Christian worship and service. In response, some of the young people planned to surprise me during my opening remarks at the rally by confronting me with a Maori dance. I got wind of all of this from a Maori youth leader who explained to me that these young people would be dancing down the aisles of the church chanting the Maori welcome.

If you have ever seen the Maori welcome, you know it could easily be misinterpreted as an array of taunting and threatening gestures. My Maori friend told me not to be shocked by it, and prepared me for it by teaching me the proper Maori response to such a welcome, utilizing the dancing gestures and the language of the Maori people.

The evening of the meeting, things unfolded just as had been predicted. When I rose to speak and took my place behind the pulpit, the back doors of the sanctuary suddenly flung open. Coming down both of the aisles were Maori young people dancing and chanting the Maori welcome. Shock waves went through the entire congregation. The young people danced up to the platform and surrounded me. They stuck out their tongues and made the wild gestures that go with the greeting. As soon as they paused, I started dancing and chanting the response I had just been taught. The Maori youth went wild with joyful excitement. A barrier had been broken! A line had been crossed!

Over the past decade, things have changed in New Zealand. Today, those white people who carry British traditions have learned to respect the Maori culture as never before and have learned to appreciate what previous generations had tried to obliterate.

13

What We Overhear about the Future

The Judeo-Christian tradition takes human history seriously. It is within the realm of history that we believe God is revealed. Furthermore, we believe that history is going somewhere, that it has a purpose to it. We believe that God is at work in the world unfolding His plan for humanity. We are marching toward the Kingdom of God that will ultimately be realized with Christ's return. Day by day we are called to work for the things of the Kingdom. We are called to try to change the world into the kind of world that God wants it to be. That is why we are called to attack poverty, racism, sexism, homophobia and the other evils that plague us. We are called to be a people who look to the future with hope.

It's Not Over

If you take a trip to Memphis, be sure to visit the Lorraine Motel. This, you may remember, is the place where Martin Luther King Jr. was assassinated. The motel has been turned into a museum about the Civil Rights movement, with special emphasis on what was happening in Memphis leading up to King's death. As you follow the course of that historical movement you end up in the hotel suite where King died and the balcony where he was shot. You see the exact spot where his wounded body expired.

As King lay dying in the arms of Andrew Young and Ralph Abernathy, Young cried out, "It's over! It's all over!"

Abernathy shouted back at him, "Don't say that! It's never over! It will never be over!"

That was, indeed, a prophetic statement. The God who worked through Martin Luther King Jr. and the Civil Rights movement will never give up on history. With our God it is never over until the Son of God returns in glory. Then the good work He is doing in us and through us will be made complete.

We Stand a Chance

There are those who say that evil is so overpowering that our efforts to combat it are futile. There are pessimists who contend that there is no way we can drive back the forces that seem to dominate our society. I disagree!

During World War II, a group of heroic men and women in France formed an underground movement that struggled against the domination of the Nazi powers. If you had been able to talk to them, you might have questioned the seeming futility of their efforts. You might have said, "How do you think you can overthrow the Nazis? Together, you are nothing but a ragtag army, poorly equipped and overwhelmingly outnumbered. You don't stand a chance against the tyrannical forces that control your nation."

They might have responded: "You don't understand! While we struggle against the forces of evil that now dominate our nation, there is a huge invasion force being assembled across the English Channel. No one knows the day or the hour when the signal will be given. But one of these days, it will be given! Then, a huge armada of ships will come across the channel and invade our country. We will join with them and they will carry us to victory!"

↵ No one knows when the Second Coming of Christ will occur. There are books, such as those by Hal Lindsey, in which the authors claim to be able to decode biblical prophecies and predict that the end is immediately at hand. Whenever I am asked to say something about the date of the Second Coming, I always answer, "I'm on the welcoming committee, not the program committee!"

So it is with those of us who struggle against the forces of darkness within history. We do so with the anticipation that on a day and an hour that no one knows, a trumpet will sound and a huge invasion force will be brought into our world, led by Christ Himself. His triumphant army will join with the church militant and carry us on to victory!

V-Day

Oscar Cullman, a Swiss-German theologian who lived through World War II, gave us a clarifying analogy for the Second Coming. He pointed out that in every war there is a decisive battle that determines the outcome of the war. After this battle, there is no question as to what the future holds. That battle establishes defeat or victory. Gettysburg was such a battle in the Civil War. Waterloo was such a battle. And in World War II it was the battle on the beaches of Normandy.

After Normandy, there was never any question as to what the outcome of the war would be. Once the Allies had established a beachhead allowing troops and arms to pour onto the continent, the fate of the Nazi armies was sealed. Nevertheless, it should be noted that more Americans died *following* that victory than died in battle prior to it. That victory, which was so decisive, did not immediately end dying among the Allied forces or suffering among the European people. The decisive battle had been fought and won on D-Day. But it wasn't until V-Day—which was a long way off—that the end of suffering and death would come.

In his analogy, Cullman makes the point that the death and the resurrection of Jesus was the decisive victory that wiped away all doubts about how history would end. After the resurrection, Christians could yell, "Christus Victor!" Christ was triumphant! The forces of darkness were defeated. Satan was overcome. But between God's D-Day on Easter Morning and that point in history when Christ returns, which will be God's V-Day, there will be suffering and pain and death. The struggle goes on! But even as we continue the struggle, we do so as people of hope. Knowing that the decisive battle has been won, we struggle against the forces of darkness with the full awareness that victory is inevitable. We wait for that victory! We wait for that hour! God's D-Day assures us of God's V-Day!

Wheat and Tares

Another parable put he forth unto them, saying, The kingdom of heaven is likened unto a man which sowed good seed in his field: But while men slept, his enemy came and sowed tares among the wheat, and went his way. But when the blade was sprung up, and brought forth fruit, then appeared the tares also. So the servants of the house-holder came and said unto him, Sir, didst not thou sow good seed in thy field? from whence then hath it tares? He said unto them, An enemy hath done this. The servants said unto him, Wilt thou then that we go and gather them up? But he said, Nay; lest while ye gather up the tares, ye root up also the wheat with them. Let both grow together until the harvest: and in the time of harvest I will say to the reapers, Gather ye together first the tares, and bind them in bundles to burn them: but gather the wheat into my barn. (Matt. 13:24–30)

I grew up in a church that had a pretty negative view of what was going on in the world. They greeted the bad news that highlighted the headlines of the daily newspapers with a certain amount of glee. When they learned that there were wars breaking out in the Middle East, they shook their heads and said these were signs of the times. When they heard of earthquakes and massive destruction in China, they said, "The end is near!" When they read the statistics of rising crime rates, the prevalence of abortion, the increase of sexual promiscuity, and the overall decline of morals, they simply smiled and said, "This is evidence that we are living in the last days!" They seemed to cheer the maladies of society, for their theology was such that they believed that the world would get worse and worse and worse until it got so bad that Jesus would have to come back to keep the world from being overwhelmed by the powers of darkness. The bleak news in the papers only assured them that we had just about reached that point.

There is some truth in what they said, for Jesus told us that there would be an increase of evil in the last days. In the parable about the wheat and the tares, He made it clear that the kingdom of evil, represented by the tares, grows greater and stronger every day. But He also made it clear that the wheat, which symbolizes God's Kingdom, also grows stronger and greater every day.

What Jesus was telling us in this analogy is that we should never be so pessimistic about history that we fail to see the positive things that God is doing. Nor should we be so optimistic about history that we do not see that the kingdom of evil is also growing in power and presence in our world. The kingdom of evil is growing up, but so is the Kingdom of God. The church will not limp out of history as a battered, beaten entity. Instead, it will march out of history triumphant! And in that final hour the kingdom of evil will be destroyed.

I remember so well being invited to the home of one of our church members on a hot Sunday afternoon. Back in those days, she was one of the few people who had an air-conditioned house. She told me to rest and take it easy while she prepared dinner. So I sat down on a special lounge chair she had in her living room. She pushed a button and the chair began to vibrate, creating a most soothing sensation. I could smell the chicken cooking in the oven—it was wonderful. The television was on and I was watching the Philadelphia Phillies trying to win the pennant.

From the kitchen, this dear woman carried on a long monologue about how we were living in the last days. And when I asked her what evidence she had that the coming of Christ was at hand, she talked about how Christians were suffering, and how that suffering was all the evidence we needed.

It was hard to grasp what she was talking about as I sat there in that vibrating chair, smelling the chicken, feeling the comfort of her air-conditioned home, and watching my favorite baseball team on television. I thought to myself, *If this is suffering . . . bring it on!*

We all know that there *is* suffering going on in the world today, and that Christians *are* being persecuted and even martyred. But amidst the evil that we see out there, we must recognize that everything is not negative. There are spiritual revivals going on around the world. There are movements to achieve social justice, more evident than ever before in history. If you look for them, there are signs of a glorious and peaceable kingdom breaking loose among us. The Kingdom of God is not only coming, but in many respects it is already growing up in the midst of us.

Got to Be a Pony

The story is told about two brothers. One was an incurable optimist and the other an incorrigible pessimist. No matter what happened to the one child, his spirits could not be dampened, and no matter what happened to the other, his spirits could not be lifted up.

One Christmas, their parents tried to exercise some correctives on these extreme attitudes. For the pessimist, they bought Christmas gifts that anticipated his every wish, hoping that seeing such an array of good things on Christmas morning would produce signs of a sunny disposition. Conversely, they would give the optimistic child nothing but a bag of horse manure.

On Christmas morning, the pessimistic boy opened a box of magnificent electric trains. In response he said with dismay, "They'll probably break." When he opened up the box containing a brand new stereo he simply groaned, "I don't have any CDs to play on this thing." He went on and on like that as he opened one gift after another. There were negative responses to everything.

On the other hand, when the optimistic child opened up his bag and found that there was horse manure in it, he started shouting and jumping up and down for joy. When his parents wanted to know what he was so happy about, he exclaimed, "Do you see what I got? Do you see what I got? There's got to be a pony around here somewhere!"

And so it is with optimists everywhere. We Christians are optimists.

No matter what they dump on us, we can stand up and say, "There's a pony out there somewhere!"

Attitudes about Death

All the talk about God's intervention in history is not enough to overcome the pain we experience when faced with the loss of a loved one. Death has a sting to it, but the good news is that the sting can be removed through Christ. In the face of death, we can declare victory.

Fathoms of Nothingness

Sören Kierkegaard has made it clear that our hyperactivism in Western society is a futile attempt to escape the awareness of death. He once wrote, "We are all like smooth, flat pebbles thrown over the surface of the pond. We dance and dance and dance along the surface until we run out of momentum, and then each of us sinks into a hundred thousand fathoms of nothingness!"

If you think that thought is depressing, try these:

"We all make noise on New Year's Eve because we are trying to drown out the macabre sound of grass growing over our graves."

Or, "We keep time with clocks instead of hourglasses. This adds to the delusion, because the hands of a clock go round and round, giving us the impression that our time goes on forever. Hourglasses constantly remind us that for each of us—time is running out!"

Death Overtakes You

The depressing concerns about death were made painfully clear to me during a classroom discussion I had with some graduate students while teaching at the University of Pennsylvania. There was a middle-aged woman in the class who was trying to earn a graduate degree in an effort to pick up her life after having been dumped by her husband of twenty-five years. As we talked about death, she remained silent for almost an hour, and then she spoke.

"You have no understanding of death," she said to the younger students. "You don't know what it's like to feel the awareness of death overtake you. I do!" She went on to say, "Imagine yourself at an organ concert, and while the organist is playing, one of the keys gets stuck. At first, you can hardly notice its monotonous groaning. Only during the pauses are you aware of it at all. But as the concert progresses, the sound of the stuck note gets louder and louder, until you hear it even while other notes are being played. Finally, the stuck note becomes so loud that it overpowers everything and the music can no longer be enjoyed. So it is with death. You are hardly aware of it at first. But as the years have unfolded for me, I have become more conscious of its overpowering presence. It grows louder and louder, and at this point in my life, it seems to dominate and drown out whatever joy there might be left."

> ～ A lady once told her pastor that she wanted to be buried with a fork in her hand. When the inquisitive pastor asked why? she answered, "When I was a little girl and we had our Christmas dinner, my mother would always say, 'Save your fork! The best is yet to come!'"

God Giveth Victory

Compare the attitude toward death expressed by that graduate student with the attitude toward death demonstrated by my father-in-law.

As Dad Davidson grew older, he suffered from hardening of the arteries. He became more forgetful and more reticent. Over the last several months of his life he said very little. He would come to dinner at our home and sit at the table, but would seldom contribute anything to the conversation. Because he was a good man, there was a benevolence in his quietude. As he sat quietly with us, it always seemed to be a peaceful smile on his face.

The day he died, my mother-in-law said that he sat up in bed, very early in the morning. He seemed to speak to an invisible presence, as he said in joyful triumph, "Oh death, where is thy sting? Oh grave, where is thy victory? Praise be to God who giveth us the victory!"

Then, he lay back in bed and died!

What a way to go! Dad had the assurance that those who die in Christ have eternal life. It is the hope we have in Him that enables us to overcome the anxieties of those who live without anticipation of the life everlasting.

Hello, God!

Joy Carroll Wallis, once an Anglican priest in Brixton, just outside of London, tells a wonderful story about a woman in her church. This woman underwent serious surgery, and because she was elderly, her prospects of recovery were slim. Fortunately, she survived the surgery.

As she opened her eyes, the first thing she saw was the blurred image of her doctor dressed in the typical white doctor's jacket. She smiled and said, "Hello, God! My name is Mary!"

That's the kind of assurance of eternal life we can all have through faith.

Not Home Yet

I heard the story of a missionary who landed in Southampton, England, after years of service in China. On the same ship was one of the leading politicians of Great Britain. That man was greeted by a cheering crowd and a marching band. He was carried off amidst the acclaim of an adoring people.

The missionary, on the other hand, got off the boat to find that there was no one there to greet him. Evidently the messages had not gotten through to those who should have been there. He sat on his luggage for several hours, but no one showed up to welcome him. He moaned and then said out loud, "God! I did not expect a marching band or a cheering crowd—but You could have had someone here to welcome me home."

The missionary said that he then heard a voice declare, "You're not home yet!"

Not All There Is

The sons of John D. Rockefeller were destined to inherit the vast fortunes of their father. However, the father wanted his sons to know what the life of the working man was really all about. To achieve that end, he insisted that they go out and work in the oil fields alongside the common laborers.

For more than two years the Rockefeller boys worked on drilling rigs. They worked long and hard hours. At the end of the workday they were exhausted and they had to endure the unpleasantness that comes from being covered with oil on a hot, hot day. At night they would sit with their fellow laborers and talk.

One day, as they were trading stories over beer, one of the Rockefellers was asked how he liked being among common workers. He responded, "I love it! This has been one of the best times of my life."

The man who asked the question said, with an edge of sarcasm to his voice, "That's because you know you're not staying. You know there is something better out there waiting for you when this is all over. You would look at things differently if you thought that working in these oil fields was all there was for you."

Likewise, the awareness that this life, with all the troubles and agonies that go with it, is not all there is alters the way in which we live. We see things differently when we recognize that there is something better out there ahead of us.

14

What We Overhear about Warnings

The Bible strikes out against hypocrisy. Jesus, especially, leaves little room for it. A holier-than-thou disposition in religious people was the target of the Lord's most intense attacks.

I'm a Gorilla

The story is told about a corporate executive who lost his job. He was so depressed that he could not go home and tell his family what had happened. Instead, he took a long walk in a park and found a bench where he could sit and bemoan his sad fate.

After a while, another man, equally depressed, came along and sat at the other end of the same bench. He looked over and saw the corporate executive with his head in his hands moaning and groaning to himself, and he could not help but ask, "What's wrong with you?"

The executive said, "I've lost my job. I can't go home and tell my family what's happened. They depend on me, and I won't be able to be the good provider I've always been. What's your problem?"

The second man said, "I run a circus and the main attraction has been a huge and threatening gorilla. People came from all over to watch that gorilla rant and rage at them. Two days ago the gorilla died, and I know my circus won't be able to survive the loss."

"Hey," said the corporate executive. "You need a gorilla and I need employment. I've got an idea. Why don't we skin the gorilla, dress me up in its skin and let me take a try at pretending. We've got nothing to lose. Why not take the chance?"

The agreement was made and the deed was done. In the days that followed, the corporate executive dressed in the gorilla's skin and raged more than the real gorilla ever had. His antics were such that the crowds coming to the circus grew larger and larger, and both men were making a fortune.

Then one day, by sheer accident, a lion ended up in the same cage with the phony gorilla. The crowds gathered to see this incredible confrontation. The lion and the gorilla circled each other as people waited to see what would happen.

Finally, the gorilla realized he was cornered and that there was no escape, and he yelled at the top of his lungs, "HELP!"

The lion shouted back, "Shut up! You're not the only one out of a job!"

Sooner or later, our pretenses are always stripped away and we are exposed for who we really are.

Did You Say This?

A friend of mine, who was pastor of a Baptist church, was once confronted by a woman in his congregation who wanted to have her seven-year-old daughter "done." By that she meant baptized.

My pastor friend was reluctant to baptize this seven-year-old girl because he wasn't sure she had had a genuine conversion. Since it is the custom of Baptists to baptize only believers, he was hesitant to accede to the woman's request. However, the woman was so insistent, that my young preacher friend knew that he had best go along with her demands.

It was the custom of this church for anyone who was going to be baptized to give a personal testimony about his or her conversion experience at the midweek prayer service. The night came when this little girl was to tell how she came to believe in Jesus and share with the congregation, in her own words, something about her Christian experience.

The little girl started by saying, "For years I wandered deep in sin . . ."

Snickers and giggles went up among the people in the small

congregation. It was pretty obvious that what she was doing was simply repeating some of the things she had heard other people say. She wasn't sharing her own faith. She was just mimicking others.

I wonder how many of us simply repeat what we have heard other people say and try to pass off the experiences of others as our own.

When Pilate asked Jesus if He really was the King of the Jews, the Lord answered, "Did you say this of yourself or did another tell you?" (John 18:34). That question needs to be asked of every one of us when we make professions of faith.

The Emperor's Clothes

We all know the wonderful story about the emperor's new clothes. Every child loves to hear about the three tailors who came to the ruler of a wealthy kingdom and told him that they could make a suit of clothes that only wise people could see. These clothes would be invisible to fools.

The king was intrigued by this idea and immediately hired the tailors, paid them huge amounts of money, and gave them everything they desired. Jewels, silks, satins, and other precious things were given to the tailors, as requests were made. The tailors, in turn, seemed to be working into the wee hours of the morning. Every time the emperor looked toward their room, he noticed that it was lit. The shadows of the tailors could be seen against the curtains. They were obviously going through the motions of sewing and making fine garments.

The king asked constantly when the suit would be completed, but he was told he would have to be patient. He paid them more and more money as the days went by, but he was growing more and more impatient.

Finally the day came when the clothes were supposed to be ready. When the king came for his fitting, the tailors *pretended* to hold up a suit of clothes. In reality, they held up nothing at all. The king saw nothing but was afraid to admit it, because the word was out that the clothes would be invisible to fools and that only wise men would be able to see them. So, the king exclaimed how much he adored the garments and how beautiful they were. All of those in the king's court made similar remarks about the clothes. No one wanted to admit that he or she saw nothing at all.

A parade was staged and the people of the kingdom lined the streets of the city, and the king, supposedly dressed in these fine garments, paraded before them. Everywhere he went people applauded and declared the clothing magnificent. Finally, one little boy blurted out, "But the king is wearing nothing! He's in his underwear!"

His mother tried to quiet him, but the boy would not be stilled. He kept on yelling that the king had no clothing at all. Other people began to confess that they, too, saw the king in his underwear. The word spread, and soon everyone was aware that they had been fooled. Most embarrassed was the king himself, who immediately sent the soldiers to arrest the tailors. Only then did he discover that the tailors had fled the kingdom with the significant wealth they had accumulated from their bogus task.

I often wonder how many people in the church say they believe things or have experienced things simply because they are afraid of what people will think of them if they tell the truth. I sometimes have to wonder, as people talk about what they feel within themselves and what they have encountered in the context of prayer, whether they are saying these things simply because they are afraid to announce that they have experienced nothing at all.

The beginning of faith is honesty about who we are and what we are, and what is going on in our lives.

Who Are You?

David Reisman and Nathan Glazr, in their classic work *The Lonely Crowd,* point out that in our modern world we are expected to play different roles with different groups of people. This alternation of roles is conducive to phoniness.

Consider the fact that I would start each day with my family at breakfast. My family cast me in the role of "Dad." They called me

"Dad" and defined me as "Dad." I would then take a commuter train into the city where I taught at the University of Pennsylvania. There I became "Dr. Campolo." I was defined as the intellectual who taught the course entitled "Existentialism and Sociologism."

In the afternoon I traveled out to the suburbs to teach at Eastern College, a small evangelical institution. There is a congeniality and informality about relationships at Eastern. In that context, I became "Tony." Titles were blown to the wind and "Tony" was the only name by which I was known. In the evening, I might go out and speak at a church. To the congregation, I would be defined as *"Saint* Anthony!"

You can understand why at the end of the day, I might stand before a mirror, look at myself, and ask, "Will the real Tony Campolo please step forward?" Having played so many different roles for so many different people, I could end up confused about who I really am. I believe that all of us in our mass society face this problem.

The solution is to allow Jesus to be the significant other in your life. In the end, you are who you are before Him! No matter where you go or with whom you associate, you should live in the consciousness of His presence and be the person He expects you to be.

Don't Tell Him

The story is told of a man who, with great regularity, would drink himself into a drunken stupor at a neighborhood bar and then stagger home, to the dismay of his wife. One night, he came home thoroughly drunk and vomited all over the kitchen floor. His wife decided she had had enough. She called the pastor of her church, who quickly came over to deal with this situation.

They carried the drunken man upstairs and tucked him into bed. Then the pastor prayed over him, saying, "Dear Lord, as you look upon this vomiting drunk . . ."

The man interrupted the pastor, and with slurred speech said, "Don't tell Him I'm drunk! Tell Him I'm sick!"

Ah, how foolish we mortals are. Do we really think that we can deceive the Almighty? We might be able to get away with our phoniness with some people, but ultimately, God knows us, with all of our warts and wrinkles.

Sooner or Later

I was once invited to speak for a church in Las Vegas, Nevada. The pastor of the church picked me up at the airport on the Saturday evening prior to my Sunday speaking engagement. As he drove me to the hotel, he went into a long tirade against gambling, citing the evil impact it had upon the city. He talked about how people who were addicted to gambling were having their lives destroyed. There was little to argue about as he described the demoralization, the prostitution, and the other forms of crime that came to the city because of gambling.

In light of what he had said, I was surprised when he took me to one of the biggest casinos in the city. When I asked him why I was staying there, he explained that the hotel rooms connected with this casino were the least expensive in town. Evidently they try to lure people to stay there by offering low rates for rooms, knowing that people who stay there are very likely to gamble there. The pastor went on to explain that taking advantage of the low rates of the hotel was good Christian stewardship, and since I didn't gamble, there should be no problem.

The next morning I went down to the lobby of the hotel at 10:15 and waited for the pastor to come and pick me up for the eleven-o'clock worship service. If you have been to Las Vegas, you know that gambling is nonstop, and the casino was very much alive at 10 A.M. As I was standing there waiting, I had my hands in my pockets, and I felt a quarter. I thought to myself, *Who comes to Las Vegas and doesn't drop a quarter in the slot machine?* We are not talking about big-time gambling here! We're only talking about one lousy quarter!

I threw the quarter into a slot machine and pulled the handle. I was hoping that the spinning disks would give me some cherries. This would indicate that I might win two or three quarters for my risk. To my amazement, up came solid black bars. I hit the jackpot!

Quarters came pouring out of the machine, landing on a brass tray that caused a loud clanging sound. A bell began to ring! It seemed very much like a fire alarm! A strobe light on top of the machine started spinning, sending out its powerful beams in all directions!

I was overwhelmed with my good fortune, and I began grabbing quarters and sticking them into my coat pockets. But as I was grabbing the quarters and pocketing them, I happened to look out the glass doors leading into the casino—and I saw the pastor!

He was coming through the doors looking for me. I didn't know what to do! I wasn't about to walk away from the fifty dollars I'd just won, but I didn't want to be seen gambling either. I crouched down and continued to pocket the quarters, all the while keeping an eye on the minister who was searching the reception area looking for me.

Finally I had all the quarters in my pocket, and the noise of the machine had died down. I figured it was okay to come out of hiding. But when I tried to stand up, I suddenly realized how heavy fifty dollars in quarters could be. It was like ten men pulling down on my coat. I took off the coat and wrapped it up with the quarters inside the pockets, then emerged to greet the pastor. He said, "It's cold outside. You'd better put on your coat. You'll freeze otherwise!"

I said, "Oh, no. I'm okay."

I got away with the deception on that occasion, but I felt guilty for a long, long time.

We all know that those who play deceptive games can get away with them some of the time, but not all of the time. Sooner or later, our sins will find us out.

15

Time to Wrap Up

There are a couple of special stories that constantly appear in my sermons. They have almost become signatures for my preaching. If any of my readers have heard me preach more than once, they undoubtedly have come across one of them. The first picks up the theme that carried us through the end of the previous chapter. It's a story about hope in the face of despair. It's the promise of victory when we feel the pain of defeat.

It's Friday, but Sunday's Comin'!

I belong to a black church in West Philadelphia. I've been a member of that church for decades, and for me, Mt. Carmel Baptist Church is the closest thing to heaven this side of the pearly gates. I preach to a lot of congregations, but I have to say that no other group of people fills me with excitement like the congregation of my home church. People in my congregation always let me know how I'm doing. Whether I am good or bad, they let me know how they feel about my message.

One time when I was preaching, I sensed no movement of the dynamism of God. I was struggling, as you have seen ministers struggle, and seemed to be getting nowhere. I had gotten about three-quarters of the way through my sermon when some lady on the back row yelled, "Help him, Jesus! Help him, Jesus!" That was all the evidence I needed that things were not going well that day.

On the other hand, when the preacher is really "on" in my church, they let him know that too. The deacons sit right under the pulpit, and whenever the preacher says something especially good, they cheer him on by yelling, "Preach, brother! Preach!" And I want to tell you that when they do that to me, it makes me want to preach!

The women in my church have a special way of responding when the preacher is "doing good." They wave one hand in the air and call out to the preacher, "Well, well." Whenever they do that to me, my hormones bubble. But that's not all. When I really get going, the men in my congregation shout encouragement by saying, "Keep going, brother! Keep going!" I assure you that you'd never hear "Keep going!" from a white congregation. They're more likely to check their watches and mumble, "Stop! Stop!"

One Good Friday there were seven of us preaching back to back. When it was my turn to preach, I rolled into high gear, and I want to tell you, I was good. The more I preached, the more the people in that congregation turned on, and the more they turned on, the better I got. I got better and better and better. I got so good that I wanted to take notes on me! At the end of my message, the congregation broke loose. I was absolutely thrilled to hear the hallelujahs and their cries of joy. I sat down next to my pastor and he looked at me with a smile. He reached down with his hand and squeezed my knee. "You did all right!" he said.

I turned to him and asked, "Pastor, are you going to be able to top that?"

The old man smiled at me and said, "Son, you just sit back, 'cause this old man is going to do you in!"

I didn't figure that anybody could have done me in that day. I had been so good. But the old guy got up, and I have to admit, he did me in—with one line. For an hour and a half he preached one line over and over again. For an hour and a half he stood that crowd on its ear with just one line: "It's Friday, but Sunday's comin'!" That statement may not blow you away, but you should have heard him do it. He started his sermon real softly by saying, "It was Friday; it was Friday and my Jesus was dead on the tree. But that was Friday, and Sunday's comin'!"

One of the deacons yelled, "Preach, brother! Preach!" It was all the encouragement he needed. He came on louder as he said, "It was Friday and Mary was cryin' her eyes out. The disciples were runnin' in every direction, like sheep without a shepherd. But that was Friday, and Sunday's comin'!" People in the congregation were beginning to pick up the message. Women were waving their hands in the air and calling softly, "Well, well." Some of the men were yelling, "Keep going! Keep going!"

The preacher kept going. He picked up the volume still more and shouted, "It was Friday. The cynics were lookin' at the world and sayin', 'As things have been so they shall be. You can't change anything in this world; you can't change anything.' But those cynics didn't know that it was only Friday. Sunday's comin'!

"It was Friday! And on Friday, those forces that oppress the poor and make the poor to suffer were in control. But that was Friday! Sunday's comin'!

"It was Friday, and on Friday Pilate thought he had washed his hands of a lot of trouble. The Pharisees were struttin' around, laughin' and pokin' each other in the ribs. They thought they were back in charge of things, but they didn't know that it was only Friday! Sunday's comin'!"

He worked that one phrase for a half-hour, then an hour, then an hour and a quarter, then an hour and a half. Over and over he came at us, "It's Friday, but Sunday's comin'! It's Friday, but Sunday's comin'! It's Friday, but Sunday's comin'!"

By the time he came to the end of the message, I was exhausted. He had me and everybody else so worked up that I don't think any of us could have stood it much longer. At the end of his message he just yelled at the top of his lungs, "IT'S FRIDAY!" and all five hundred of us in that church yelled back with one accord, "BUT SUNDAY'S COMIN'!"

That's the Good News. That is the word that the world is waiting to hear. That's what we have got to go out there and tell the world's people. When they are psychologically depressed, we have to tell them that Sunday's coming. When they feel that they can never know love again, we've got to tell them that Sunday's coming. When they have lost their belief in the miraculous so that they no longer expect great things from God, we must tell them that Sunday's coming.

We must go to a world that is suffering economic injustice and political oppression and tell them that Sunday's coming. The world may be filled with five million hungry. Half of the planet may be under the tyranny of communist domination. Dictators may rule in Latin America. People may find their rights abridged and their hopes under attack. But I am not ashamed of the gospel of Christ, because to all of those who are on the brink of despair, I can yell at the top of my lungs, "IT'S FRIDAY, BUT SUNDAY'S COMIN'!"

The Agnes Story

If you live on the East Coast and travel to Hawaii, you know that there is a time difference that makes three o'clock in the morning feel like nine. With that in mind, you will understand that whenever I go out to our fiftieth state I find myself wide awake long before dawn. Not only do I find myself up and ready to go while almost everybody else is still asleep, but I find that I want breakfast when almost everything on the island is still closed—which is why I was wandering up and down the streets of Honolulu at three-thirty in the morning, looking for a place to get something to eat.

Up a side street I found a little place that was still open. I went in, took a seat on one of the stools at the counter, and waited to be served. This was one of those sleazy places that deserves the name "greasy spoon." I mean, I did not even touch the menu. I was afraid that if I opened the thing something gruesome would crawl out. But it was the only place I could find.

The fat guy behind the counter came over and asked me, "What d'ya want?"

I told him, "A cup of coffee and a donut."

He poured a cup of coffee, wiped his grimy hand on his smudged apron, then grabbed a donut off the shelf behind him. I'm a realist. I know that in the back room of that restaurant, donuts are probably dropped on the floor and kicked around. But when everything is out front where I could see it, I really would have appreciated it if he had used a pair of tongs and placed the donut on some wax paper.

As I sat there munching on my donut and sipping my coffee at three-thirty in the morning the door of the diner suddenly swung open, and to my discomfort, in marched eight or nine provocative and boisterous prostitutes.

It was a small place and they sat on either side of me. Their talk was loud and crude. I felt completely out of place and was just about to make my getaway when I overheard the woman sitting beside me say, "Tomorrow's my birthday. I'm going to be thirty-nine."

Her "friend" responded in a nasty tone, "So what do you want from me? A birthday party? What do you want? Ya want me to get you a cake and sing 'Happy Birthday'?"

"Come on!" said the woman next to me. "Why do you have to be so mean? I was just telling you, that's all. Why do you have to put me down? I was just telling you it was my birthday. I don't want anything from you. I mean, why should you give me a birthday party? I've never had a birthday party in my whole life. Why should I have one now?"

When I heard that, I made a decision. I sat and waited until the women had left. Then I called over the fat guy behind the counter and I asked him, "Do they come in here every night?"

"Yeah!" he answered.

"The one right next to me, does she come here every night?"

"Yeah!" he said. "That's Agnes. Yeah, she comes in here every night. Why d'ya wanna know?"

"Because I heard her say that tomorrow is her birthday," I told him. "What do you think about us throwing a birthday party for her—right here—tomorrow night?"

A smile slowly crossed his chubby face and he answered with measured delight. "That's great! I like it! That's a great idea!" Calling to his wife, who did the cooking in the back room, he shouted, "Hey! Come out here! This guy's got a great idea. Tomorrow's Agnes's birthday. This guy wants us to go in with him and throw a birthday party for her—right here—tomorrow night!"

His wife came out of the back room all bright and smiley. She said, "That's wonderful! You know Agnes is one of those people who is really nice and kind, and nobody ever does anything nice and kind for her."

"Look," I told them, "if it's okay with you, I'll get back here tomorrow morning about two-thirty and decorate the place. I'll even get a birthday cake!"

"No way," said Harry (that was his name). "The birthday cake's my thing. I'll make the cake."

At two-thirty the next morning I was back at the diner. I had picked up some crepe paper decorations at the store and had made a sign out of big pieces of cardboard that read, "Happy Birthday, Agnes!" I decorated the diner from one end to the other. I had that diner looking good.

The woman who did the cooking must have gotten the word out on the street, because by 3:15 every prostitute in Honolulu was in the place. It was wall-to-wall prostitutes . . . and me!

At 3:30 on the dot, the door of the diner swung open and in came Agnes and her friend. I had everybody ready (after all, I was kind of the MC of the affair) and when they came in we all screamed, "Happy Birthday!"

Never have I seen a person so flabbergasted . . . so stunned . . . so shaken. Her mouth fell open. Her legs seemed to buckle a bit. Her friend grabbed her arm to steady her. As she was led to one of the stools along the counter we all sang "Happy Birthday" to her. As we came to the end of our singing, "Happy birthday, dear Agnes, Happy birthday to you," her eyes moistened. Then, when the birthday cake with all the candles on it was carried out, she lost it and just openly cried.

Harry gruffly mumbled, "Blow out the candles, Agnes! Come on! Blow out the candles! If you don't blow out the candles, I'm gonna hafta blow out the candles." And, after an endless few seconds, he did. Then he handed her a knife and told her, "Cut the cake, Agnes. Yo, Agnes, we all want some cake."

Agnes looked down at the cake. Then without taking her eyes off it, she slowly and softly said, "Look, Harry, is it all right with you if I . . . I mean is it okay if I kind of . . . what I want to ask you is . . . is it okay if I keep the cake a little while? I mean is it all right if we don't eat it right away?"

Harry shrugged and answered, "Sure! It's okay. If you want to keep the cake, keep the cake. Take it home if you want to."

"Can I?" she asked. Then looking at me she said, "I live just down the street a couple of doors. I want to take the cake home and show it to my mother, okay? I'll be right back. Honest!"

She got off the stool, picked up the cake, and carrying it like it was the Holy Grail, walked slowly toward the door. As we all stood there motionless, she left.

When the door closed there was a stunned silence in the place. Not knowing what else to do, I broke the silence by saying, "What do you say we pray?"

Looking back on it now it seems more than strange for a sociologist to be leading a prayer meeting with a bunch of prostitutes in a diner in Honolulu at three-thirty in the morning. But it just felt like the right thing to do. I prayed for Agnes. I prayed for her salvation. I prayed that her life would be changed and that God would be good to her.

When I finished, Harry leaned over the counter, and said, "Hey! You never told me you were a preacher. What kind of church do you belong to?"

In one of those moments when just the right words came, I answered, "I belong to a church that throws birthday parties for whores at three-thirty in the morning."

Harry waited a moment, then he answered, "No you don't. There's no church like that. If there was, I'd join it. I'd join a church like that!"

Wouldn't we all? Wouldn't we all love to join a church that throws birthday parties for whores at three-thirty in the morning?

Well, that's the kind of church Jesus came to create! I don't know where we got the other one that's so prim and proper. But anybody who reads the New Testament will discover a Jesus who loved to party with whores and with all kinds of left-out people. The publicans and "sinners" loved Him because He partied with them. The lepers of society found in Him someone who would eat and drink with them. And while the solemnly pious could not relate to what He was about, those lonely people who usually didn't get invited to parties took to Him with excitement.

Our Jesus was and is the Lord of the party. This book is an attempt to make that point blatantly clear. It is an attempt to highlight an often-forgotten dimension of what Christianity is all about: The Kingdom of God is a party!

Afterword

A lot of my stories have been taken from the experiences of those who work alongside me in ministry. Over the past thirty years I've been privileged to develop and lead the Evangelical Association for the Promotion of Education. This is a missionary organization that is committed to creating programs to help the poor in Third World countries, as well as providing an array of programs for teenagers and children in at-risk neighborhoods across the United States and Canada.

Our affiliated programs are touching the lives of thousands of kids daily. Our heroic young missionary volunteers accomplish more through the grace of God than anyone could imagine, but they need your help. Could you pray for our work, and if possible, could you join in that family of financial supporters that is so essential to keeping our missionaries on the field? Here is an overview of what we're doing.

EAPE/Kingdomworks is a Christian missionary organization that creates educational, medical, and economic development programs among disadvantaged people in Third World countries, as well as urban America. In all that we do, we seek to partner with indigenous church leaders in efforts to express God's love in words and deeds.

In 1997 we initiated our newest program called **Mission Year**. Through this ministry, we have deployed several teams of young missionaries to work with inner-city churches on both the East and West Coasts for a year of door-to-door visitation and community service.

Another of our programs, **UrbanPromise**, is located in Camden, New Jersey, reaching more than fifteen hundred children and teenagers during our peak season. This ministry reaches kids through a variety of activities that include Bible study, evangelism, tutoring, sports, music, and drama. This past year, a new elementary school was started, as well as an alternative school for junior-high and senior-high young people.

In Philadelphia, EAPE/Kingdomworks has created **Cornerstone Christian Academy.** This is a rigorously academic elementary school that serves children from low-income neighborhoods. We have an outstanding faculty, an array of volunteers, and a student body of more than three hundred students. This school stands as a beacon of hope in one of the most desperately at-risk communities in America.

EAPE/Kingdomworks has extensive work in Third World countries. **Beyond Borders,** our program in Haiti, has partnered with Haitian church leaders to create seventy-five literacy centers for adults and children. Without a doubt, this ministry is touching the lives of some of the neediest people in the world, generating among them hope for the future along with personal confidence. In the Dominican Republic, we have been involved in creating and supporting the Evangelical University of the Dominican Republic and the Technical University of the South.

In Zimbabwe, an estimated 35 percent of the population will die from AIDS. Already there are thousands of children who have lost both parents to this dreaded disease, and they themselves are infected with the deadly HIV virus. Working with our British affiliate, **Oasis,** we are providing care for these desperate children, so that they can live and die with dignity.

I would be very appreciative if you would give to these ministries. Our address is

Evangelical Association for the Promotion of Education (EAPE)
Box 7238
St. Davids, PA 19087
Tel: 610-341-5962
Fax: 610-341-4372

Contact us either by mail or by connecting with our Web site which is: www.tonycampolo.com

Perhaps you are interested in becoming a volunteer or a full-time missionary with us. You may want more information about our ministries. Or, perhaps you would like to know about other books and tapes that we have available. All of us at EAPE welcome your inquiry, and I personally would appreciate hearing from you.

Sincerely,
TONY CAMPOLO
August 2000

Notes

1. J. D. Salinger, *Franny and Zooey* (Boston: Little, Brown, 1961).
2. Arthur Miller, *Death of a Salesman* (New York: Bantam Books, 1951).
3. Thornton Wilder, *Our Town: a Play in Three Acts* (New York: Coward-McCann, Inc., in cooperation with S. French, Inc., New York, 1939).
4. C. Austin Miles, "In the Garden." P.D.
5. Sir Thomas More, "Believe Me When All Those Endearing Young Charms." P.D.

ADDITIONAL SELECTIONS
FROM TONY CAMPOLO

Best-selling author and popular speaker Tony Campolo challenges believers to find fulfillment in learning how to seize the day! With contagious enthusiasm, he invites us to rediscover the wonder and joy of life, love, and dreams through a renewed passion for God.

"This is a book about a way of doing business that works," says author Campolo. "It is a refutation of those cynics who claim the values and principles laid down in the Bible mitigate against success in the dog-eat-dog world of commerce and industry." An ethical, biblical approach to business for a more satisfying and fulfilling career.

With candor and insight, Tony Campolo passionately hits on hot button issues that impact the Christian life, including how to: protect yourself from technology without becoming Amish, have a devotional life without becoming a monk, and figure out the will of God without hearing voices from Heaven.

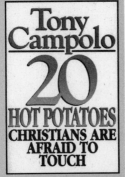

AIDS, women preachers, public schools, psychological counseling, homosexuality, and working mothers—these are some of the hot issues that many Christians avoid discussing. With insight and clarity, Tony Campolo confronts today's toughest social and moral questions and raises a few of his own.